MEDIACTIVE

ISSUE 2 ▸ Celebrity

Editor
Jonathan Rutherford
email: j.rutherford@mdx.ac.uk

Editorial Office
Mediactive
Media, Communications and Cultural Studies Group
Middlesex University
White Hart Lane
London N17 8HR

Advertisements
Write for information to Mediactive
c/o Barefoot Publications
99a Wallis Road
London E9 5LN

Collection as a whole copyright Mediactive 2003
Individual articles copyright the authors 2003

Text setting: E-type
Cover Design: Fran Davies

Website www.barefootpublications.co.uk

Editorial Board

Clare Birchall	Media and Cultural Studies, Middlesex University
Anita Biressi	Cultural and Media Studies, University of Surrey, Roehampton
Helen Cunningham	Media and Cultural Studies, Middlesex University
Lynda Dyson	Media and Cultural Studies, Middlesex University
Jeremy Gilbert	Cultural Studies, University of East London
Gary Hall	Media and Cultural Studies, Middlesex University
Dorota Kolodziejczyk	English Department, University of Wroclaw
Jo Littler	Media and Cultural Studies, Middlesex University
Heather Nunn	Cultural Studies, University of Surrey, Roehampton
Jopi Nyman	Department of Foreign Languages, University of Joensuu
Roger I. Simon	Centre for Media and Culture in Education, University of Toronto
Imre Szeman	Institute of Globalization, McMaster University, Canada.
Joanna Zylinska	Media and Cultural Studies, University of Surrey, Roehampton.

Contents

Editorial
The opposite of fame   4

Jo Littler
Making fame ordinary: intimacy, reflexivity and 'keeping it real'   8

Oscar Reeves
Cheriegate! Celebrity, scandal and political leadership   26

Anita Biressi and Heather Nunn
The especially remarkable: celebrity and social mobility in reality TV 44

Matt Hills
'Subcultural celebrity' and cult TV fan cultures   59

Kay Dickinson
Pop stars who can't act   74

Jeremy Gilbert
Small faces: the tyranny of celebrity in post-Oedipal culture   86

Guidelines for Contributors   110

Notes on Contributors   111

Editorial

The opposite of fame

John O'Farrell's novel *This Is Your Life* tells the story of thirty-something Jimmy Conway who, near the beginning of the book, describes the dawning disappointment of living a non-celebrity life:

> As you grow older, you gradually realise that the gulf between where you are now and where you had hoped to be is never going to be bridged. In your daily life you pretend that you will catch up, make up all that lost ground and suddenly be catapulted to that elusive magical place called 'Success'. But slowly it starts to seep through from your subconscious to the conscious: this is your fate, this is who you are, *this* is your life.[1]

Jimmy wants fame because it 'wouldn't just bring status and respect and money and purpose. It would mean an end to being so bloody lonely all the time' (p199). Humiliated by being confronted with letters he wrote as a teenager, letters advising his future self how to handle his fame, he suddenly finds himself pretending that he *is* famous and faking the persona of a semi-famous stand-up comedian. Inevitably, however, when he does accede to celebrity status, it doesn't make him fulfilled (p225). Lazy journalists recycle each other's quotes and perpetuate the myth of his celebrity through the stardom-machine whilst he feels increasingly isolated and friendless. The desirable spaces and glittering pleasures that only celebrities have access to suddenly seem hollow, shallow, empty. He always wondered what was behind that door on the set of his favourite breakfast TV programme. Now he knows: there is nothing behind it.

The novel's happy ending sees Jimmy turning his back on celebrity and revaluing the locality of his life and his friendships. His friends forgive him and produce their own surprise version of the TV show *This Is Your Life* in his local pub. His life is no longer a famous life but a friend-filled life and because of that it is better, richer, more successful. Like Ben Hatch's book *The Lawnmower Celebrity* – in which the anti-hero's high-achieving BBC dad pays more attention to his celebrity friends than his son – *This Is Your Life* is a story of a young, white British man coping badly with not being famous against all his expectations.[2] In part both books might be read as dramatising a crisis of the certainties of Britishness, and of white male masculinities. At the same time they dramatise shifts in formations of celebrity culture. Journalist Barbara Ellen writes of how our culture has spawned the existence of 'willabees' rather than 'wannabees' – a generation for whom there is a moment of *expectation* that you will be famous rather than merely hoping or wanting to be famous.[3] Some of this structure of feeling is easy to recognise. When I was at primary school I distinctly remember feeling that whatever it was I was doing at one particular moment would look embarrassing when it was my turn to appear on *This Is Your Life*, an event which my six-year old self confidently expected to happen (whereas, of course, the only thing that turned out to be embarrassing is the structured expectation of that incident itself).

These examples indicate that how lives are evaluated – what they are imagined as being, and what they are imagined as being *worth* – can be formed in relation to what 'celebrity' is thought to be, and to involve. We draw boundary lines between so-called 'ordinary' lives and the 'extraordinary ordinariness' of celebrity culture, and the unevenness of the power relations between a celebrity and a non-celebrity is only too graphic.

This second issue of *Mediactive* explores some of the ways celebrity functions now in relation to 'ordinariness' and to contemporary versions of democracy (or to the lack of it). What does the surge of commentary, programming and statements of fascination – 'ironic' or otherwise – about celebrity say about the culture we live in? How might we understand the dynamics of power, the *politics* of contemporary forms of celebrity, and its relationships to ordinary lives? Where might we look to find the more positive aspects of celebrity, if there are any – and if not, where might we look to pursue alternatives?

The contributors approach these issues by drawing from a range of areas including cultural studies, sociology, politics, film studies, philosophy and media studies. Drawing from the latter, Heather Nunn and Anita Biressi interrogate the dramatic rise of 'Reality TV' in Britain and the instant fame granted to some of its participants. They explore how Reality TV has increasingly allowed for the rise to celebrity status of those who have neither cultural capital nor elite roles in the public sphere, and examine how these 'classed' subjects become iconic through their newly found social mobility.

Jo Littler's piece investigates how a Blairite 'meritocracy' has enabled new possibilities for social and cultural mobility, but argues that it has at the same time allowed inequalities to become polarised in new ways. It considers how this is both reflected in and produced by celebrity culture, examining the recurrent use of three tropes: intimacy, reflexivity and 'keeping it real'. These are considered in order to explore how desiring fame is in itself constructed as desirable and rendered 'ordinary'.

Oscar Reyes explores the relationship between New Labour and celebrity by focusing on Blair's persona. Prime ministers have tailored their images to play on their 'ordinariness' for a long time: Wilson through beer and sandwiches, Thatcher by being simply a grocer's daughter, Major by accentuating his unexceptionalness, Blair through semi-faded jeans and mugs of tea. Reyes examines how in the case of Blair, this ordinariness has been primarily articulated to the family. Examining the centrality of 'trust' in New Labour politics, he shows how these issues are not debated in terms of work or institutions, but around the celebrity family, which has become both a crucial mechanism to secure power and also that which threatens to break it down.

Different types or *modes* of celebrity culture are discussed by Kay Dickinson and Matt Hills. Kay Dickinson's starting point is the enthusiastically vitriolic response to pop stars who crossover into film. The outrage at 'pop stars who can't act', she argues, reveals conservative value systems which aim to keep workers in their place. At the same time, however, she points out that such categories of worth appear to be changing: celebrity all-rounders (like the 'all-conquering brand' Jennifer Lopez) are multi-tasking in different fields. The article explores what our reactions to celebrity work reveals about the intertwined issues of celebrity and regimes of labour.

Pointing out that celebrities have often been taken as being ubiquitous, as known by everyone, Matt Hills suggests we think about how they might not always act to sustain a common, unifying currency, but how they have other functions, such as connecting subcultures of fans. Proposing that we think about 'subcultural celebrity', he looks at the popular theorising of two dramatic comedies, the Hollywood movie *Galaxy Quest* and the made-for-BBC-TV film *Cruise of the Gods*. Both invent their own cult TV series and worlds of subcultural fandom, and both engage in a mixture of parodying, reinforcing and/or subverting cult TV fans' images as 'sad, weird geeks'. Hills examines how these texts negotiate the issue of fans' cultural power, and considers what this can tell us about the potential *range* of relationships between celebrities and their audiences.

Finally, Jeremy Gilbert rethinks how we might understand the relationship between celebrity, social life and individuality. He points out that conventional psychoanalytic accounts of the relationship between stars and their fans (like much neo-Lacanian political theory) reproduce the assumptions of early twentieth century mass psychology, and can be challenged by a range of theoretical and empirical sources, from the work on the productivity of fan cultures to the deconstructions of psychoanalysis offered by Deleuze and Guattari and Mikkel Borch-Jacobsen. He argues that celebrity culture is inherent to capitalism from its earliest emergence and that there is a fundamental incompatibility between capitalist individualism and any form of meaningful democracy.

There are many links between these pieces, which share a concern with how changing celebrity cultures relate to issues of power, equality and democracy. One link is the interest in the *affective* investments and relationships between celebrities and 'ordinary people'. Another is the concern to explain the significance of dramatisations of the route from ordinary to extraordinary. In different ways the contributors all explore how celebrity is both a magnified example of the individualisation of our society and a key mechanism through which this process of individualisation functions. Alongside celebrity, then, this issue of *Mediactive* is keen to consider its opposite, or opposites, whether thought of as 'the ordinary', as non-fame, as a fan, as community, as socialism or as anti-individualism. To do this is to move beyond the individualistic dreams of celebrity, to move from stating 'This is your life!' to asking: 'What are our lives?'

Jo Littler
Issue editor

Notes

1. John O'Farrell, *This Is Your Life*, Doubleday 2002 p57.
2. Ben Hatch, *The Lawnmower Celebrity*, Indigo 2000.
3. Barbara Ellen, 'Who'd wannabe a willabee?', *The Observer Magazine*, 10 February 2002, p3.

Special Subscription Offer

Subscribe to Mediactive now – £24 for three issues – and you will receive a free copy of the book *Art of Life, Essays on living, love and death*, edited by Jonathan Rutherford (includes essays by Zygmunt Bauman, Ulrich Beck, Adam Phillips, Madeleine Bunting).

To subscribe, send your name, address and payment (cheque or credit card, made payable to Lawrence and Wishart), stating which issue you wish to start with, to:

Mediactive, L&W, 99a Wallis Road, London E9 5LN.

Or email subs@lwbooks.co.uk

Making fame ordinary
Intimacy, reflexivity, and 'keeping it real'

Jo Littler

In our contemporary 'meritocratic' culture new possibilities of social and cultural transition are being produced alongside sharp inequalities of wealth and status. This article considers how this situation is both reflected in and produced by celebrity culture. It does so by examining three common tropes that are currently generated around celebrity: intimacy, reflexivity and 'keeping it real'. These three tropes are examined together as examples of how desire for fame is both constructed as desirable and rendered 'ordinary'.

>You better lose yourself in the music, the moment
>You own it, you better never let it go
>You only get one shot, do not miss your chance to blow
>This opportunity comes once in a lifetime yo [1]

In the lyrics to Eminem's *Lose Yourself* fame is not simply something that anyone talented can get if they work hard enough. The moments when it might pay off to strive are few and far between: celebrity is a chance moment, a fleeting conjunction, something necessary to seize because of its rarity. You mess up the moment and you will be back in the place you came from, the place to which you do not wish to return. Fame here is not merely the inevitable outcome of the diligent buffing up of some 'raw talent'. It is not quite the low-risk Protestant celebrity work ethic offered by *Fame Academy*. Eminem's lyrics express a society in which celebrity is more of a random, and potentially cruel, lottery than a birthright for the righteously dedicated. They figure the fragility of fame; they articulate a sense of slim pickings, a place from which there are not many chances, a world in which it becomes all the more important to recognise and to channel intense energy into taking those chances up. In part the intensity comes out of this sense that it is as easy to lose everything as it is difficult to gain it.

Besides aggrandising a singular moment of chance, *Lose Yourself* displays many other motifs that are recurrent in our present mode of celebrity culture. Firstly, it invites us to get very intimate with the emotions of a celebrity, in this case a conflation of the hero of the film *8 Mile*, to which these lyrics are soundtrack, whose character is a semi-fictionalised representation of Eminem, the celebrity who plays him. Secondly, both film and song are highly reflexive about the business of being a celebrity, offering commentaries on some of the 'rules' of the game. And thirdly, they focus on the moment just *before* becoming famous: presenting this moment of graft, of striving, of desire, as a moment of raw 'realness', of authenticity. (In this case the 'authenticity' is also obviously gained through its articulations with, and appropriations of, 'black' cultures.[2]) In this paper I want to consider these three themes – 'real' pre-fame, intimacy and reflexivity, not in order to 'explain' Eminem's *Lose Yourself*, but rather, using it as a starting point, or a springboard, to consider the entrenched cultural currency of these themes beyond this specific instance. In particular, I want to examine how these tropes contribute to constructing the desire for fame and to making it seem 'ordinary'.

To do this, to begin with, we need to say a little about celebrity culture in relation to wider dynamics and contexts of social and cultural power. One of the most useful ways to begin to think these issues through is to draw on Nick Couldry's work on media power and its relation to 'the ordinary'. Couldry writes that

> By 'media power', I do not mean the power (ideological or otherwise) exercised upon us by specific media texts; I mean more generally media institutions' differential symbolic power, the concentration of symbolic power in media institutions: that is, the fact that we take it for granted that the media have the power to speak 'for us all' – indeed to define the social 'reality' that we share – a power which individuals, corporations, pressure groups, professional bodies and even perhaps the state do not have.[3]

Couldry draws from Bourdieu, from Sennett and Cobb's theories of the hidden injuries of class, and from his own interviews with 'ordinary' people (who indicated that being on television made them feel 'empowered') to argue that there is a constructed symbolic boundary between 'the media world' and 'the ordinary world'. If the former is marked by authority, he argues, the latter is marked by a lack of validation, and it is in the gap between them that the 'hidden injuries of media power' are formed. Clearly, this leaves us with some very useful tools with which to think about the hidden injuries of celebrity as well as media power. Towards the end of his article Couldry does point us in this direction, arguing that programmes like *Big Brother*, in which 'ordinary' people become celebrities, do not so much transcend the division between worlds as work to reinscribe it. 'To put it crudely', he writes, 'why else would the transition to celebrity (and the games played in celebrity's border zones) matter so much?'.[4] In Couldry's terms, media celebrity therefore becomes a means of symbolic validation, a way to 'really' exist, to mean something in public and private, to be rich with symbolic as well as material capital. To seek the full glare of celebrity media validation is to strive against the hidden injuries of disempowerment; to strive against the symbolic disempowerment of the 'ordinary'.

Of course we are not particularly used to thinking of not-being-a-celebrity in the potentially hyperbolic and victimised terms of 'an injury'. But Couldry's schema is extremely useful as it names a phenomenon and a scale that has different levels of intensity. Viewed in this way, it resonates with other academic and critical understandings of the relationship between celebrity, media and society. David Morley, for example, summarises Suzanne Moore's observation that talk shows can demonstrate 'the simple but powerful capacity of the media to offer these participants some form of recognition, however perverse, of their existence'.[5] The importance of recognition is not confined to a few; as Chris Rojek writes:

> To some extent, the dynamics of modern society mean that all of us are caught up in the celebrity race. It is axiomatic that only a minority acquire the public acclaim and recognition that we associate with celebrity status. It is also axiomatic that if the majority suffer from feelings of rejection and invalidation, they internalize them in ways that pose no threat to the social order.[6]

In other words, what Rojek calls rejection and invalidation, what Moore/Morley might term a lack of recognition and what Couldry calls 'injuries' have a lot in common. Whether at the extreme (e.g. Barry George, obsessed since his poverty-ridden childhood with ways of achieving fame, and trying to find it by killing TV presenter Jill Dando) or 'normal' (e.g. feeling not quite as 'successful' as a celebrity but not minding) end of the spectrum, these strategies of cultural coping or non-coping indicate a society and a culture that has developed some extraordinarily unequal ways to validate people's sense of self and collective worth.

If celebrity culture can be understood in terms of symbolic disempowerment, it also needs to be understood in the context of economic and social disempowerment: in terms of unequal access to material resources and social mobility. Here we need to consider the character of the political conjuncture we inhabit in terms of the Blairite *vision* of Britain as a 'meritocracy'. A 'meritocracy' is nowadays understood as 'a social system which allows people to achieve success proportionate to their talents and abilities, as opposed to one in which social class or wealth is the controlling factor'.[7] This is part of the wider frame of post-Fordist late capitalism in which relatively rigid class identity distinctions have to some extent fractured and multiplied.[8] Whilst the routes between class stratifications have become marginally more porous – generating some high profile examples – substantial class mobility remains out of reach for the majority. Divisions between wealth have become exacerbated over the last few decades in particular, to the extent that in London 43% of children are now living in poverty.[9]

Crucially, the Blairite vision is not of an equality of wealth (as under 'old' Labour) but rather of a state that will facilitate the ability to strive for it. As with the logic of late capitalism more broadly, this implicitly rests on the proposition that it is only possible for a few people to be really 'successful'. At the same time, however, the structural drive of Blairite policies, as with other neo-liberal governments like the US, has been to increase marketised competition and to further the dismantling of the welfare state, resulting in the attempted destruction of collective provision and the erosion of basic quality provision for the poor. This has exacerbated the inequalities of opportunity from which 'talent' (in itself a problematic enough concept) can be healthy enough, culturally equipped enough or even well-fed enough to 'rise' through the cultural and social pool. In other words, even taken within its own terms, this discourse of meritocracy fails. That people do not surface at the top through 'merit' alone is easily illustrated in the US context by the nepotistic career of the current president. As the supportive structures of social welfare institutions become impoverished, people shoulder the burden and threats of social insecurity on an increasingly individualised basis, in what Ulrich Beck describes as 'the risk society'.[10] The lottery becomes a core motif for our times.

The increasing disparity between rich and poor, the risky lottery of social opportunity and the lack of cultural validation for many people in our society goes some good way to explaining the expansion of interest in celebrity culture and the eagerness with which opportunities to become one are taken up and consumed. These are some of the wider contexts in which Eminen's hymn to the fleeting moment of potential for fame is produced, in which it is bought by the truckload, and in which it clearly resonates with broader structures of feeling. *Lose Yourself* offers the image of immersion in the moment of opportunity for fame. Risk everything to lose your old self and your lack of validation; gamble your identity to acquire wealth, to become acknowledged, to become somebody.

Keeping it real: Cinderella and the celebrity work ethic

Getting to know 'the real' or 'inner' person behind or inside the celebrity has for a long time been an integral means of generating interest in them. As Richard Dyer pointed out in *Heavenly Bodies*:

> Stars are obviously a case of appearance – all we know of them is what we see and hear before us. Yet the whole media construction of stars

encourages us to think in terms of 'really' – what is Crawford really like? Which biography, which word-of-mouth story, which moment in which film discloses her as she really was? The star phenomenom gathers these aspects of contemporary human existence together, laced up with the question of 'really'.[11]

The question, the enigma of 'really' is partly what generates the cultural and economic turnover of our fascination with celebrities. It sells them, products about them, and products tenuously connected to them. It informs the way we connect to celebrities, whether as abstract friends; or offering us glimpses of what we would like to be; of lifestyles we wish to inhabit; or spaces of impossible longing, characteristics against which we measure ourselves, or mechanisms through which we bond with other people.[12]

However, this question, of what celebrities are 'really' like, can matter in a range of different ways. From psychoanalytic perspectives, asking the question of what a celebrity might 'really' be like might indicate needs or desires felt to be lacking from our own lives or psyches. From post-structuralist perspectives, it could indicate an unhealthily essentialist fetishisation symptomatic of Western logocentricism, rather than tracing multiple, interrelated developments, intensities or 'realities'. In terms of cultural history, the search to find out what celebrities are 'really' like could be understood in the context of the rise of Romanticism, possessive individualism and capitalist modernity. Such a search to find out who and how celebrities 'really' are has been an integral motor of the celebrity machine for a long time. The leaking of celebrity secrets has been a long-standing promotional tactic used in order to produce 'authentic' information that, as Dyer points out, is 'often taken to give a privileged access to the real person of the star'.[13]

Dyer's elegant and lucid analyses of film stars such as Judy Garland, Paul Robeson and Marilyn Monroe spawned a whole generation of film studies students who wrote essays on the construction of a particular star's image and fame. In his earlier book, *Stars*, Dyer influentially wrote that 'what is interesting about them is not the characters they have constructed [...] but rather the business of constructing/performing/being (depending on the particular star involved) a "character"'.[14] Reading this today, and thinking about this in a wider context from that of solely film stars, it is clear that it is not only academic and journalistic commentators who find the business of constructing celebrity fascinating. Celebrity reflexivity, or mulling over the business of being or becoming a star, has become a conspicuous preoccupation of stars themselves, as *Lose Yourself/8 Mile*, along with a wide range of other cultural examples, indicates. Take for example the lyrics Craig David sings with older 'star' Sting on a recent track about the *Rise and Fall* of celebrity. Partly presented as smug autobiographical triumph ('I always said that I was gonna make it/Now it's plain for everyone to see') the lyrics also function as a parable on the vagaries of the star system which 'naturally' entail the 'rise and fall' of the star.[15] Loosely, the narrative tells of a self who celebrity changed, making him 'too concerned with all the things I own' and 'blinded by all the pretty girls I see', leading to a loss of 'integrity'. Integrity is signified by monogamy, by wanting rather than having riches, by learning the rules of the game (presumably from Sting) and by being nice to and appreciating the power of the fans, from whom the lyrics beg forgiveness. What is interesting to note about *Rise and Fall* is the combination of reflexivity about the business of being a celebrity, emotional interiority and self-criticism on offer: this is a celebrity confessional.

The markers of what makes a celebrity authentic here are the presentation of emotional intimacy with the audience, alongside a degree of reflexivity about being in the position of a celebrity, and an ability to reference the legitimate 'moment before' fame. It is a similar story to *American Life* in which Madonna sings of how forgetting her 'original' motivation, she 'lost herself' after becoming a star. Again, the moment *before* becoming a celebrity is positioned as the 'authentic' moment, of the real 'her' that can be re-occupied. The lyrics of the chorus cut between tenses, between this retrospective comment and presenting the experience of trying to become a celebrity in the present tense, a moment quavering with instabilities: 'Do I have to change my name?/Will it get me far?/Should I lose some weight?/Am I gonna be a star?'. The subjectivity that is aspiring to be a star, presented as their position and that of their listeners, is the position that is coded as being 'real'. To examine such productions of celebrity 'normality', such messages of how they, once, inhabited the position of wanting to be a celebrity *too*, and why they hold such purchase in our culture, might work not so much to explore how celebrities are 'just like us' through the way they magnify 'everyday' mannerisms or characteristics (that is, what Couldry terms elsewhere their 'extraordinary ordinariness') but rather to think about how they are presented as being like us *in wanting to be celebrities*. For the idea that 'to be ordinary' in our culture will probably entail 'wanting to be a celebrity' in part gets reproduced and naturalised from such positions.

Clearly, referencing 'the moment before' fame is in part about money, work and class. This has been blatantly dramatised recently in the lyrics, video and reception of *Jenny from the Block*. In the video, Jennifer Lopez and her 'real-life' fiancé Ben Affleck are shown going about their everyday lives, caught on a montage of different types of film. The framing of the images codes the relationship between 'the lovers', and between J-Lo and the viewers, as playful and intimate. We get a glimpse of what happens beyond the 'official' definition of the frame: we are offered a peek into the celebrity world. Simultaneously, we witness the moment of the 'framing itself': we are invited into J-Lo's line of vision, her subjectivity. Again, the idea of 'intimacy' is being sold to us. The world of press and photography is depicted as being unreal, as external to the relationship we as viewers have with J-Lo. And again it also offers us up another type of 'real' apart from intimacy. 'Keeping it real' means remembering what it was like *before* being wealthy.

Her name changed to the homely 'Jenny', the artist formerly known as J-Lo tells us that despite her enormous wealth, she's still the same old down-to-earth girl from round the corner in the hard streets of the Bronx that she always was. It mobilises one of the most common celebrity stories: the celebrity who worked his or her way up from the bottom of the social pile. The rags-to-riches tale is an age-old narrative. It is the story of Cinderella, whose basic plot elements, as Angela Carter said, 'occur everywhere from China to Northern England', wherever there is social inequality;[16] but with different meanings according to the time and place, whether they be amusing pastimes for the Viennese bourgeoisie or expressions of wish-fufilment for the Irish poor. That this currency has become prominent today is not particularly surprising considering that we live in a world in which rags have become more prevalent and riches more opulent. At the same time the narrative is inflected in some very modern ways. Instead of merely luxuriating in her palatial excess, Cinderella now has to show that she can still remember that she started out in the kitchen. This knowledge or awareness structures her character; it stops her 'getting above herself', it keeps her 'real'.

Why this is such a motif in contemporary culture can be understood in relation to the neo-liberal discourse of meritocracy. Of course, just as there is plenty right in wanting people to move beyond experiences of deprivation, there is nothing wrong with not wanting to be arrogant or socially snobby (and such sentiments have become common sense in a way they weren't even fifty years ago). But as Stuart Hall pointed out many years ago, celebrations of 'the popular' can take many different political forms.[17] And this is not a populism which, in its appreciation of 'working class' people and forms, wants to hold this up and celebrate it in order to try and give them more opportunities and resources. J-Lo's ditty and image is not about what she gives back: it's what she has extracted from the street – her 'realness', her supposed urban 'groundedness' – and has *taken away with her* that's important. It is a structure of feeling that uses its 'appreciation' for the block for entirely individualistic purposes, in order to justify enormous wealth and divest itself of any guilt, rather than to enter into a reciprocal relationship. As such it sustains, furthers and deepens inequality rather than tackles it, and is entirely congruent with what has been called 'corporate populism'.[18] What more perfect image could there be for a company to use to sell, what more potent dream to buy than glamour which pretends to be democratic through-and-through?

In J-Lo's case there are of course important explanatory reasons we can bring in here in terms of gender and 'race'. It has long been recognised that cultures of ostentatious wealth are ways for disenfranchised people to stick two fingers up to those who held them down and back. Nowhere perhaps is this more apparent than in the thick heavy gold chains of black rappers, sported also by young white working class boys who share their material and cultural disempowerment (and who often want to borrow what is perceived as being their hyper-masculinity).[19] It is apparent in one feminist discourse that, since the shoulder-padded working girls of the 1980s at least, has trumpeted ostentatious wealth as a signifier of female liberation. J-Lo offers a similar celebration of a materialist young feminism as the Destiny's Child anthem *Independent Women*, which celebrates 'all the honeys / that make the money'. On these collective grounds it is not surprising that a Latino singer from the Bronx might be attracted to *bling*.

But acknowledging these moves as resistant does not mean that they are progressive or emancipatory. As Don Slater has pointed out, there is a fine but deeply significant line between acknowledging that a consumer or a culture is 'active', and assuming that it is 'oppositional'. To trace the story of the confusion between them is to trace one of the stories of cultural studies, and in between these positions there is 'the most powerful insight of the whole tradition, that cultural studies is part of a social process of making social sense'.[20] This example like many others offers one type of liberation (e.g. gender equality) only by annexing or connecting it to a celebratory endorsement of the profit motive of consumer capitalism. Whereas some used to think that black struggles and gender struggles were by themselves opposed to capitalism (and they often were, as the people on the top of the pile were wholly, instead of mainly, dominated by the white, the male and the upper class), today it is clear that they are not. As Sheila Rowbotham, the campaigner for women's liberation from the 1960s, poignantly puts it: 'our hopes have been appropriated, our aspirations twisted'. Identity politics became articulated to the corporate search for profit as well as the search for co-operation:

> Ironically, openings created by social movements were to present market opportunities – the slogans transmogrified into designer labels and some quick-footed 'alternative' capitalists emerged from the melee. Yet the radical dream of the sixties was to be stillborn, for we were not to move towards the cooperative egalitarian society we had imagined. Instead the sixties ushered in an order which was more competitive and less equal than the one we had protested against.[21]

Paul Gilroy talks of a similar process as 'filleting', a process by which corporate interests gut a progressive discourse 'for what they want and adapt it to the rhythms of their own complicity with consumerism'.[22] It highlights the importance of linkages, or articulation: of how discourses can be linked, re-appropriated or co-opted for progressive or negative ends (in other words, to promote equality, co-operation and the sharing of power and resources, or to promote inequality, individualism, and the waste and uneven distribution of power and resources) and how discourses build their power through alliances. If we are looking for what Williams called 'resources of hope', or, in a more contemporary sense, meanings that can be rearticulated to more progressive ends, one might be in the widespread ridiculing of J-Lo's sentiments of being able to 'keep it real' despite her wealth. She clearly is not the same as she was when she was much poorer, and, to many, the inability to recognise this is insulting to both those who do live in conditions of material poverty and to the intelligence of her audience. It appears disingenuous. As Dorien Lynskey put it in a review in *The Big Issue*: 'she claims on Jenny from the Block that she's just the same girl she always was, which either means (a) she was demanding all-white dressing rooms with matching flowers as a 12-year old in the Bronx, or (b) she's talking bollocks.'[23] Or as a student, Feben Iyassu, said to me in a seminar, how can she really still be 'Jenny from the Block' when she doesn't give anything back? In part it is because the song and video goes out of its way to highlight this contradiction, that it makes the faultline in the logic only too transparent. But it also offends because it offers little affective sense of the *difficulty* of moving out of such social circumstances. In effect, the narrative of individualist advancement is the same as that offered by Eminem – who is much more rarely decried for it – but without the brooding sense of the riskiness and precariousness of material and social advancement, or the downside to living on the block.[24]

Clearly, what Lopez offers is not the only type of relationship that is articulated between celebrities and their materially poorer 'roots'. In the video for *It takes more*, for example, Ms Dynamite rejects a glossy video set for an estate, singing with local people, unlike Jenny who uses 'the street' as a vehicle to show off her individualised success and beauty to them. The visual narrative is not only about Ms Dynamite, but about other people, such as a little boy watching gangsta rap on video; the lyrics engage with broader social issues about racism and economic deprivation, and they are about more people than just the singer. There are a lot of messages that are less individualistic and more co-operative, analytical and progressive at work. It is still the case of course that Ms Dynamite's is still represented as an *individualised* achievement, for whilst there are aspects of some celebrities that can be used or articulated in less unequal ways, structurally, celebrity is always by definition individualistic.[25] Celebrity is both a magnified example of the individualisation of our society and a key mechanism through which this process of individualisation functions. This raises important questions about whether and how celebrity can ever be used to further equalities, and if not, what the opposite or alternatives to celebrity might be. As the Ms Dynamite example shows, there are clearly many ways in which celebrities are used to promote discourses that benefit 'the collective good'. The pronouncements celebrities have made, the attitudes they embody and the identifications they make possible can all be used to instigate cultural change that engenders equality rather than exploitation. For example, from the suffragettes to the Spice Girls and beyond many different types of feminisms have been promoted through celebrities. Non-governmental organisations are perennially keen to garner celebrity support as they raise the news profile of an issue and engender affective identifications.

The most obvious contemporary model of 'democratic' celebrity is probably the celebrity of the 'leader' of the Zapatistas in Mexico, Subcommandante Marcos. Masked and anonymous, this is a celebrity who everyone and anyone can claim to be, as no-one knows who he 'really' is. This is a self-consciously dissolved model of celebrity in which Marcos is everyone, sharing the fame like that other model of celebrity where celebrity is dissolved into the populace, *Spartacus*. Stanley Kubrick's well-known 1960 epic about slave emancipation (penned by a blacklisted screenwriter) famously featured other male slaves taking in solidarity the identity of condemned revolutionary Roman slave-turned-hero, so that one and all became a shared identity ('I am Spartacus!). Analogously, the recent finale of *Buffy the Vampire Slayer* dissolved Buffy's celebrity and power into all and any potential slayers.

Yet of course in another way these are not so much 'alternative' models of celebrity but rather its antithesis, in which the celebrity is also eradicated by being dissolved into the collectivity. In 'Letter to a Harsh Critic' Deleuze terms 'the opposite of celebrity' as a set of liberated singularities, opening a 'self' up to the multiplicities within:

> It's a strange business, speaking for yourself, in your own name, because it doesn't at all come with seeing yourself as an ego or a person or a subject. Individuals find a real name for themselves, rather, only through the harshest exercise in depersonalization, by opening themselves up to the multiplicities everywhere within them, to the intensities running through them. A name as the direct awareness of such intensive multiplicity is the opposite of the depersonalization effected by the history of philosophy: it's depersonalization through love rather than subjection. What one says comes from the depths of one's ignorance, the depths of one's own underdevelopment. One becomes a set of liberated singularities, words, names, fingernails, things, animals, little events: quite the reverse of a celebrity.[26]

In these Deleuzian terms, to be the opposite of a celebrity is to not seek individual fame, to not emphasise individuality, but to dissolve such individualism and open ourselves up to the multiplicities that constitute us.

Within the constraints of the celebrity framework of individualism, the Ms Dynamite example does at least offer less individualistic messages. However, whilst restricted by its mode, it remains the case that there is still the gap between the ordinary and celebrity worlds, a disjunction in power which is attempted on some level to be compensated for by the emphasis on the moment before fame through returning to it as the 'real' moment of emotional grounding.

Up close and personal: emotional intimacy

Anchoring the celebrity's image in relation to a 'real moment before fame' invites us to feel closer to celebrities and to suggest our proximity to their emotions. This also needs to be understood in relation to a broader context of the rise of celebrities' emotional literacy and the intensification of the intimacy we are invited to feel with their feelings. Perhaps nowhere is the rise of celebrity intimacy demonstrated more baldly, or literally, than through the title of the British weekly glossy magazine, *Closer*. Launched by EMAP in late 2002, *Closer* aimed to rival the other main celebrity weekly *Now* and to build on the sales success of EMAP's celebrity magazine *Heat* (aimed at a younger target audience) by being pitched at women from their late twenties to early fifties.[27] The plan was to revitalise an older and 'more traditional' women's magazine market with a shot of youthful celebrity culture. Its subtitle '[*Closer*] to the people making the news THIS WEEK' does not, unsurprisingly, feature newspaper editors or politicians, but showbusiness celebrities together with the quasi-sensational true-life stories of 'ordinary' people.

Closer is just one title within what has become termed the 'celebrity magazine market'. Whilst magazines obviously used celebrity coverage before, the scale and title given to this market is indicative of the noticeable expansion of celebrity culture more generally, and its title is indicative of one of the key forms this is currently taking: a suggestion that we are getting more intimate with or 'closer to' celebrity lives than ever before. As P. David Marshall pointed out in *Celebrity and Power*, celebrities have been a site through which the private sphere has been dragged into the public for a long time.[28] However, the current insistence on increased emotional intimacy might also be thought about in relation to broader social and cultural changes. Here I am thinking in particular about changes in business and organisational cultures and to the rise of 'soft capitalism'. Nikolas Rose has persuasively outlined how, whereas previously organisations had been environments with 'defensive norms such as mistrust, conformity, and power-centred competition', from the 1970s they were encouraged to emphasise 'striving for information, collaboration, facilitation, openness, trust, risk-taking, shared responsibility, choice, learning, open competition'. The 'emotional, more primitive side of human nature' could be harnessed in order to create individuals have been taught to manage, self-actualise and govern their own success.[29] Business began to use the power of 1960s collective and self-help.

Gesturing towards 'holistic' models, this business model relies on a greater degree of closeness – or intimacy – between colleagues than traditional atomised hierarchies. What has come to be called 'soft capitalism'[30] harnesses informality, emotion, relationships, cultural bonds, culture and creativity to produce economic success. This works both on the level of the workplace, whether by paying attention to organisational cultures, to the cultural bonds between staff or by introducing forms of leisure and 'play'. At the weaker edge of soft capitalism, this might mean dress-down Fridays and office parties; at the more extreme (and softer) end, it can mean the lack of hierarchies and collectivist hedonism epitomised by the St Lukes advertising agency, working together in creative ways for private profit. There is clearly a close connection here between intimacy and informality, and the rise of both might also be interpreted in relation to what is commonly understood as the 'decline of deference' in the post-war (WW2) period.

Such an emphasis on intimacy and on emotional organisational cultures is also part of soft-capitalism in terms of the relationship between an organisation and its customers. Getting to know your post-Fordist niche market has bred an intense emphasis about knowing intimate details about your customers in the Anglo-American world in particular. As the best-selling business book *Customer Intimacy: Pick Your Partners, Shape your Culture, Win Together* puts it:

> Like scores of today's like-minded market leaders around the world, they are on the cutting edge of the most important strategic transfomation of the decade: the shift to customer intimacy. They've abandoned the old us-versus-them mind-set to embrace a single common insight: the largest source of growth, advantage and profit resides in the design and development of intimacy with customers.[31]

Again, the language of sixties and seventies co-operativism is co-opted to produce big bucks for corporate business. It is in this context that the premium placed on intimacy and emotional literacy might be considered. Seeing celebrities outside of the traditional places and spaces in which it is acceptable to inhabit celebrityhood – in either ordinary or extraordinary contexts – has been a key part of the appeal of the spate of many recent celebrity reality TV programmes. Displacing the celebrity from its natural habitat became a way to foreground their emotional responses (and 'real' behaviour), whether in the Australian jungle (*I'm a celebrity – get me out of here!*) or the big house in east London (*Celebrity Big*

Brother). It is a way to generate interest in 'other sides' of their characters, to present us with new ways of getting intimate with them.

What this engenders is a kind of premature celebrity confessionalism. There have always been gossip and scandals, interviews and confessions around celebrities. But unlike the 'heavenly bodies', perhaps, about whom nuggets of information are revealed through interviews, and who are subject to the usual barrage of scandalous gossip, we now have many stars who appear only too keen to tell us *very early on* in their careers about how they are unheavenly and how they have dirty emotional closets to clean out. There is a rush to bring out celebrity autobiographies at increasingly young ages (Geri Haliwell and David Beckham, to name but two); Eminem's 'Cleaning out my closet' contains characteristically coruscating reflections on his personal history ('I got some skeletons in my closet and I don't know if no one knows it. So before they thrown me inside my coffin and close it, / I' ma expose it.').

Such productions of 'closeness' and intimacy with stars can be connected to the increase in 'intimacy' across a variety of media genres. Surveying the history of DIY shows on television, for example, Charlotte Brunsdon noted the recent move towards close-ups and jokey, high camp melodrama.[32] Such images can attempt to narrow the visual and emotional distance from the audience. Whilst predictably such productions of this kind of visual/emotional intimacy are often most pronounced in traditionally 'feminine' areas, they can also be seen in more male-dominated realms, with for example the rise of less deferent and aggressive TV interviewing styles that are more intimate by being more 'invasive'. We might locate such moments of intimacy in relation to what David Morley, drawing on Raymond Williams, terms 'the relationship between distance, familiarity and alienation'.[33] The apparent rise in intimacy, whether coded through visual close-ups, lack of linguistic deference, or the presentation of 'private secrets' can, sometimes, in many ways clearly act as compensation for that simultaneously old-fashioned and hideously modern condition of alienation.

Intimacy and emotional literacy in our culture might be thought in relation to the similar position to the double-edged gains and losses of the feminisation of industry. They are both issues around which it sometimes becomes easy to scapegoat 'feminisation' rather than to disentangle the relations between gender, identity politics and late capitalism. Emotional literacy has become a way not only to improve relationships but to feed commercial profit. Obviously emotional literacy doesn't have to be articulated to the search for private profit. For example, the campaigning organisation for emotional literacy, Antidote, has an economic policy stating that 'societies marked by sharp inequality cannot thrive' and stating that it wants to work towards seeing money 'flowing through society in ways that can improve the quality of life for everybody within it'.[34]

Reflexivity and irony

The rise of reflexivity in general has been taken as a key characteristic of our culture for some time now; as Lash and Urry put it in *Economies of Signs and Space*, '... it is only in late modernity (or postmodernity) that aesthetic reflexivity comes to pervade social processes'.[35] In the mid-1990s, reflexivity seemed to hold for some commentators like Anthony Giddens the promise of liberation from the shackles of oppressively hierarchical traditions. In more circumspect and ambivalent vein, Scott Lash, John Urry and to a certain extent Ulrich Beck considered how reflexive subjects could entail either potentially more liberatory possibilities or they could be articulated to new regimes of capital accumulation (or both).[36]

Being reflexive is important both for the interpellated celebrity audience, and, if we think back to the lyrics above, for many celebrities 'themselves' (or, in other words, their celebrity personas). Whereas the Madonna and Craig David examples appear to mull over the precariousness of celebrity and their occasional inability to always *manage* it in the best possible way, Eminem's lyrics and presentation tend to foreground the performance of celebrity (for example, through the title of his album, *The Eminem Show*). To whatever degree, such reflexivity indicates a celebrity-system in which the stars have to be more attuned to an audience that is assumed to be increasingly media-savvy and more aware of the rules of the celebrity game. Other points on the celebrity spectrum of reflexivity might include more 'ironic' celebrity consumption marketed to an audience interpellated as extremely 'wised-up' to the rules of the celebrity game. The magazine *Heat*, for example, is often sold through this premise. It is marked by less reverence towards celebrities in general (a strategy designed to appeal to its young UK audience and which has in sales terms succeeded, resulting in the creation of a US variant).

Heat is marked by not wanting to keep its celebrities on the pedestals installed by *Hello!* or *OK!* and to demonstrate irreverence towards the position of celebrities. (Such irreverence is more widespread, palpable in other media such as the commentaries of *The Mirror*'s 3am girls). It also offers a subject position based around 'ironic' distance from the whole celebrity game. To some extent it shares this with the BBC game *Celebdaq* in which the audience bets on the stocks and shares of celebrity currency, offering us a similar meta-commentary on celebrity as a game with rules. *Heat*'s advertising campaigns ironise the social rules of the celebrity 'game' and our interactions with it. They ironise desire for celebrity gossip; they poke fun at its social role as a channel for discussion in a work context; they even highlight and laugh at the connection between female gossip about celebrities and emotional intelligence. In this respect it might be compared to the kind of hyper-reflexivity used in the advertising industry, where ironic youth advertising became a staple of the campaigns for Diesel and Benetton, although in this case the strategies are being deployed with a less 'high art' and more overtly populist, at times even bawdy, touch. Ironically, even when articulated through ironic distance, these practices are enabling an audience to feel 'closer to' the secret lives of celebrities. It is what might be called, after Foucault, an 'incitement to discourse' around celebrity intimacy.[37] It is a discourse of critical and cynical distance about the celebrity-machine, a critical discourse that is predominantly channelled straight back into feeding it, to the reforming and the reselling of celebrity, rather than the dissolution of it.

At the same time, such reflexivity over the 'game' of celebrity can also be interpreted in terms of the changes in hierarchies of cultural value. Previously, for professional middle-class taste-makers, engaging with the gossip and tittle-tattle around celebrity culture was positioned as downmarket, flashy, sensationalist and trashy: as 'common'. Now, to know about it is important, even if this is accompanied by a vestigial sense of distance through irony. Knowing about celebrity culture is sold to us as a way of appearing democratic and populist, of appearing disengaged from social snobbery, of appearing socially and culturally fluid: to have the potential to engage with a wide range of people across different social layers and backgrounds. Such skills are important ones to have in order to be a member of the professional middle classes in our network society.

Of course audiences interpret such texts in a variety of ways. As so many cultural studies texts from the 1980s worked hard to tell us – and as, importantly, and not coincidentally, *Heat* is keen on telling us too – the audience is not made up of a bunch of passive dupes. Clearly the ways these texts, these products, these messages about celebrities, intersect with a myriad of different daily lives is phenomenally multiple and diverse. They can offer us points of reference for our own lives. Celebrities offer us not only 'role models' (or the lack of them) but examples of lives and responses lived in a culture that has some similarities to ours, even if the similarities are only in terms of temporality, gender or a shared status as 'individuals'. As Dyer pointed out '… what makes them [stars] interesting is the way in which they articulate the business of being an individual, something that is, paradoxically, typical, common, since we all in Western society have to cope with that particular idea of what we are. Stars are also embodiments of the social categories in which people are placed and through which they have to make sense of their lives'.[38] They offer us ways to be 'ourselves' and to of connecting us to other people.

These are some of the ways such narratives and discourses operate and engage us. In one way it is not useful to cut ourselves off from celebrity culture. It saturates so much of cultural life that to not know what is going on or how it works is not particularly possible. Neither is it desirable if we want to learn about how our culture works or to connect to other people. But at the same time it is important to interrogate what is going on and in whose interests. Is it really 'ours'? To what ends are we putting our interests, our money and our energies? Is the celebrity dream really equal? And, more difficultly, where do we invest our energies when we know it's not an equal dream? *Heat* plays on the possibilities of such knowledges. After all, there might seem to be few obvious places to put your energy in our culture if you know a celebrity culture is an unfair culture (although there are in fact many places that might be less obvious to some: NGOs, the Social Forum Movement, alternative medias, community and not-for-private-profit organisations ...[39]). Reading *Heat* provides one outlet in which by reading it you can register your criticism, your cynical awareness and your knowledge of how the celebrity system works, even if, unfortunately, its neo-liberal postmodern reflexivity does channel such potential back to the realm of inequalities rather than to the redistribution of some of its concentrations of power.

Sometimes those relations of power are more inadvertently explicit than others. The TV advert for *Closer* depicted a female office worker miniaturised and sitting on a shelf in a cupboard, where she witnesses a scandal unfolding. She is a metonym for the magazine and its readers. *Closer*, the advert says, will offer the reader a much more intimate relationship to what is going on in public. She is presented as canny, obtaining knowledge, finding out what's really going on. But it does not bring the reader 'closer' in order to interact with these events that are deemed as important. It is not an intimacy that is reciprocated in any meaningful sense. In terms of emotional intimacy, this is a *one-way* relationship in which continual disempowerment is embodied through the woman's size.

In our contemporary 'meritocratic' culture, new possibilities of social and cultural transition are being produced alongside sharp inequalities of wealth and status. This is a situation that is both reflected in and produced by celebrity culture. In such a context, intimacy, reflexivity and dramatising the 'grounded' moment of pre-fame are key tropes through which current celebrity culture is reproduced and maintained. They are ways or expressions through which a desire for fame is itself constructed as desirable and is rendered 'ordinary'. Intimacy can be offered to the audience or fan as a possible way of legitimating themselves by investing in the celebrity world. For celebrities, it can be a way of connecting and persuading people that they have something in common and divesting themselves of their role in creating that disjunction in power. Reflexivity can be a way for celebrities to reach a more media-savvy audience and for audiences to attempt to disengage themselves from the sphere of celebritydom even whilst they may be reinforcing it. And being 'grounded', or holding on to the symbolic rags, can be used to generate identifications, to articulate the decline of snobbery and to attempt to assuage guilt over the social inequalities of our lottery culture. All three are currently in widespread circulation. All three are ways of making fame seem ordinary, when of course, unless we are all receiving the same material and symbolic recognition, it is no such thing.

Notes

Thanks to Jonathan Rutherford and Lynda Dyson for advice and encouragement.
All websites accessed July 2003.

1. The full lyrics from this and other songs quoted in this article can be found at a range of online lyric sites such as http://www.azlyrics.com/c.html.
2. To discuss this would require a whole paper to itself. There has been much media commentary over how Eminem uses 'black culture' to gain credibility. See for example Kimberley Chabot Davies, 'White Hip-Hop: Keepin' it Real or Keepin' it Political?' in *Politics and Culture*, Issue 3, 2003, http://aspen.conncoll.edu/politicsandculture/; Michael Moore, *Stupid White Men*, Harper Collins 2001, p.66, or http://www.misanthropic-humanist.org/0702.htm. For a discussion of the tradition of white music artists using the 'authenticity' of black rap as a means of 'keeping it real', see Tricia Rose, *Black Noise: Rap Music and Black Culture in Contemporary America*, Wesleyan University Press 1994; William Eric Perkins (ed), *Droppin' Science: Critical Essays on Rap Music and Hip Hop Culture*, Temple University Press 1996; Susan Gubar, *Racechanges: White Skin, Black Face in American Culture*, Oxford University Press 1997.
3. Nick Couldry, 'The hidden injuries of media power', in *Journal of Consumer Culture*, Vol 1 No 2, November 2001, pp155-177. See also his *The Place of Media Power: Pilgrims and Witnesses of the Media Age*, Routledge 2000.
4. Ibid, p172.
5. David Morley, *Home Territories: Media, Mobility and Identity*, Routledge 2000, p111.
6. Chris Rojek, *Celebrity*, Reaktion Books 2001, p147.
7. Michael Young coined the word 'meritocracy' in his book, *The Rise of the Meritocracy 1870-2033*, Penguin, 1958. He later claimed Blair was woefully misusing it. See Michael Quinion's article on his website *World Wide Words* for a discussion of the changing meanings of the word 'meritocracy': http://www.quinion.com/words/topicalwords/tw-mer1.htm.
8. On post-Fordism see for example David Harvey, *The Condition of Postmodernity*, Basil Blackwell 1989.
9. Greater London Authority, *London Divided: Income Inequality and Poverty in the Capital*, GLA 2002.
10. Ulrich Beck, *The Risk Society*, Sage 1992.
11. Richard Dyer, *Heavenly Bodies: Film Stars and Society*, Macmillan Press 1986, p2.
12. See for example Matt Hills *Fan Cultures*, Routledge 2002 or David Gauntlett, *Media, Gender and Identity*, Routledge 2002.
13. Dyer, *Stars*, New edition; British Film Institute, 1998, p61.
14. Ibid.
15. My discussion of these lyrics is considering them in relation to wider discourses; if it were considering them in relation to music cultures, or considering their wider significance as part of the song, then their sonic and somatic effects would have to be taken into account.
16. Angela Carter, 'Introduction' to Angela Carter (ed), *The Virago Book of Fairy Tales*, Virago 1990.
17. Stuart Hall, 'Notes on Deconstructing the Popular', in Raphael Samuel (ed.), *People's History and Socialist Theory*, Routledge and Kegan Paul 1981.
18. For a discussion of Anthony Barnett's use of this term and related themes see Michael Rustin, 'The New Labour ethic and the spirit of capitalism', in *Soundings*, Issue 14, Spring 2000, p116.
19. For a useful discussion of this see Kimberley Chabot Davies, 'White Hip-Hop: Keepin'

it Real or Keepin' it Political?' in *Politics and Culture*, Issue 3, 2003, http://aspen.conncoll.edu/politicsandculture/ accessed October 2003. See also Tricia Rose, *Black Noise: Rap Music and Black Culture in Contemporary America*, Wesleyan University Press 1994.
20. Don Slater, *Consumer Culture and Modernity*, Polity Press 1997, p171.
21. Sheila Rowbotham *Promise of a Dream: Remembering the Sixties*, Penguin 2000, ppxiv-xv.
22. Marquand Smith, 'On the State of Cultural Studies: An interview with Paul Gilroy' *Third Text* 49, Winter 1999-2000, p21.
23. Dorien Lynskey, 'How Lo can you go?', *The Big Issue*, December 2-8, 2002, p29.
24. But a good example is Johann Hari, 'Eminem: the president's friend', *Independent on Sunday*, 12 January 2003.
25. See Dyer, 1986, op cit, ppix-18 on celebrities, society and individualism.
26. Gilles Deleuze, 'Letter to a Harsh Critic', in *Negotiations 1972-1990*, Columbia University Press 1995, pp6-7.
27. Ciar Byrne, 'Emap brings celebrity title Closer', *Media Guardian*, 12 September 2002.
28. P. David Marshall, *Celebrity and Power: Fame in Contemporary Culture*, Minnesota University Press 1997.
29. Nikolas Rose, *Governing the Soul: the Shaping of the Private Self*, Second edition, Free Association Books 1999, pp114-116.
30. Paul Heelas, 'Work ethics, soft capitalism and the "turn to life"', in Paul du Gay and Michael Pryke (eds), *Cultural Economy*, Sage 2002, pp78-96.
31. Fred Wiersema, *Customer Intimacy: Pick Your Partners, Shape Your Culture, Win Together*, Harper Collins 1998.
32. Charlotte Brunsdon, 'Taste and time on television', *Media times/historical times* symposium, Goldsmiths College, 25 May 2003.
33. Morley, op cit p179.
34. http://www.antidote.org.uk/html/economy.htm accessed 20 April 2003.
35. Scott Lash and John Urry, *Economies of Signs and Space*, Sage 1994, p54.
36. Ulrich Beck, Anthony Giddens and Scott Lash, *Reflexive Modernization: Politics, tradition and aesthetics in the modern social order*, Polity 1994.
37. This phrase is used in terms of the 'incitement to discourse' around sexuality – i.e. that the Victorians didn't so much clamp down on thinking and talking about sexuality as much as multiply it. Michel Foucault, *The History of Sexuality Vol 1*, Penguin 1978.
38. Dyer, 1986, op cit, p18.
39. For example, NGOs such as the World Development Movement (http://www.wdm.org.uk/); alternative media such as Indymedia (www.indymedia.org) or Mediachannel (www.mediachannel.org); community organisations such as LETS (www.gmlets.u-net.com) or TELCO (www.telcocitizens.org.uk). The European Social Forum Movement is on-line at www.fse-esf.org, and the World Social Forum Movement is discussed in Hilary Wainwright, *Reclaim the State*, Verso 2003 and Paul Kingsnorth, *One No, Many Yeses: A Journey to the Heart of the Global Resistance Movement*, Free Press 2003.

Cheriegate!

Celebrity, scandal and political leadership

Oscar Reyes

This article interprets the Cheriegate scandal of December 2002 in light of the wider political importance of trust and the Blair family image. The Blairs are projected as a hard-working family, and the 'extraordinary-ordinariness' of this position is the premise upon which identification with the Blair leadership is built. In this respect, the Blairs have more in common with other celebrities than is often realised.

The Cheriegate scandal of December 2002 was 'the saga of the prime minister's wife, the conman and the topless model turned lifestyle guru.'[1] For more than two weeks the tabloid press unearthed a constant stream of revelations about the Blairs' financial dealings and introduced the reading public to an extraordinary cast of Cherie Booth's (or Blair's) 'weirdo pals.'[2] We found that Cherie was hopelessly dependent on Carole Caplin, a former soft-porn model with a psychic mother who assisted the prime minister's wife in her communications with the spirit world.[3] We read that Cherie stood naked in the shower while Caplin scrubbed the 'toxins' from her back.[4] And we learnt that she took financial advice from Peter Foster, Caplin's partner and a convicted fraudster, when buying two Bristol flats for her son Euan. Number 10 'lied repeatedly in an attempt to cover up his involvement' – a symptom, we were told, of the culture of spin and sleaze corrupting the heart of government.[5] In sum, Cheriegate had sex, money and the abuse of power – all the ingredients of a good scandal… except one. Remarkably, all of this coverage was achieved without the added inconvenience of any obvious wrongdoing.[6]

If we examine the Cheriegate saga strand by strand its scandalous nature starts to unravel. The *Mail on Sunday*, which broke the story on 1 December 2002, initially claimed that the Blairs 'used a notorious fraudster to buy them two luxury flats at a knockdown price.'[7] But the Blairs paid the same amount as other purchasers of similar properties. The same newspaper's claims about attempted stamp duty evasion, about Cherie Booth's role in helping to rehabilitate Peter Foster's reputation and about his role as her financial adviser also turned out to be untrue. Allegations that the Blairs had misused their blind trust, set up to shield them from conflicts of interest, were dismissed by a senior civil servant. The Conservatives talked of a potential violation of the ministerial code, but no substantive evidence was ever produced to back up this claim. The further scandal of Cherie's intervention in Peter Foster's deportation case also turned out to be unfounded. When Cherie Booth made an emotional television statement on 10 December, she did admit to two mistakes – a misunderstanding with the Prime Minister's press office, and an unwise decision 'to allow someone I barely knew and had not then met to get involved in my family's affairs.'[8] But there was nothing earth-shattering in these revelations. As *The Times* noted, her behaviour 'should be deemed unwise, but she has not crossed the "improper" line, let alone an 'illegal' threshold.'[9]

Faced with this litany of lies, half-truths, insinuations and distortions, it would be tempting to interpret the Cheriegate scandal as a symptom of the trivialisation of public life, or as a further nail in the coffin of journalistic integrity. Cheriegate *was* a distraction from the serious issues of the day, obscuring the Blair government's 'accumulating failure to deliver on public services,' not to mention its escalation towards an immoral and illegal attack on Iraq.[10] It was also a clear instance of the bias and agenda-setting capabilities of the right-wing press – a 'naked political assault on the government by its declared enemies led by the *Mail*', as Polly Toynbee put it.[11] I will not be arguing against these interpretations, but I do want to suggest that they overlook what was really at stake. Cheriegate was, above all, a crisis of the Blair family's integrity. It was an attack upon the trustworthiness of Cherie Blair and, by association, Tony Blair himself. And it was also an attempt to undermine the marketing projection of the Blairs as an ordinary hard-working family.

For present purposes, the effectiveness of these attacks is of secondary importance. What I want to focus on, instead, are the mysterious circumstances in which such a trivial story can appear to matter. I will argue that the Cheriegate case reveals the importance of trust, personality and family image to the construction of Blair's political leadership. British Prime Ministers can no longer rely on the auspices of that office as a guarantee of their legitimacy and, as a result, we must grapple with a new context for thinking about their leadership. The emergence of a presidential dimension to British politics brings personality and family image to the centre, because they provide the basis upon which citizens can identify with the leader as 'one of us'. Contemporary leadership values this (extraordinary) ordinariness over charisma or heroics and in this respect it is significantly indebted to the norms of a media culture that celebrates celebrity. As Blair himself puts it, 'I think I function better as a politician *because* I lead such a normal life'.[12]

The 'convergence in the source of power between the political leader and other forms of celebrity' has not yet been studied by British political scientists.[13] This article starts from scratch, therefore, by highlighting the role that 'identification' plays in securing an *affective* investment in politics. Particular attention is paid to the role of the Blair family in the marketing of New Labour. The Blairs are projected as an ordinary hard-working family, and this constitutes the 'ideal' subject position from which to view New Labour discourse. This family-centred identification also serves as the bedrock upon which 'trust' can be built. Trust is important to New Labour politics – not so much for sociological reasons as for expressly political ones. In the run up to the 1997 election, Labour modernisers emphasised trust as an antidote to perceived Conservative 'sleaze,' and sought to articulate its meaning to a set of pledges designed to appeal to 'ordinary' (i.e. middle-class) families. But the emphasis on trust, and its projection through the character of Blair himself, has also left New Labour vulnerable to 'decapitation strikes' aimed at Blair, his family and his spin-doctors. The Cheriegate scandal is a prime example of this. It was an attempt to undermine the Blairs' reputation in order to undermine the Blair government. Viewed in these terms, the Cheriegate scandal's twin focus on trust and family integrity begins to make sense – whether or not the scandalmongers and protagonists consciously recognised what was at stake. The Cheriegate case, and the varied responses to it, also help us to make sense of the dynamics of British political leadership as a whole.

Celebrity, identification and British political leadership

Traditional interpretations of British political leadership focus on the 'office of the Prime Minister'.[14] Crudely speaking, the legitimacy of this office is viewed as the product of a longstanding institutional set-up, which is occasionally given a boost by a sudden and ungentlemanly outbreak of charisma. This view has been vigorously challenged in recent years, however, by talk of presidentialisation, which basically means a qualitative shift away from collective government towards centralised leadership.[15] The office of the Prime Minister is seen as less institutionalised and 'far more dependent upon the individual incumbent for its meaning and effect.'[16] A by-product of this is that the leader's personality has become an increasingly important object of public scrutiny, with the result that political marketing is correspondingly focused upon the leader's ability 'to be the emblematic and substantive personification of party principles and priorities.'[17]

The presidentialisation thesis draws attention to the increasingly central role played by leaders' personalities, which it interprets as a product of both sociological changes in the boundary between public and private, and changes in the way politicians interact with the media. But it offers very few resources with which to understand the impact of personality. I will argue that we must understand identification if we are to assess the impact of leaders' personality, and that an understanding of the 'ordinary-extraordinary' status of celebrities can help in this task.

'Identification' is the operation through which political subjects are created and revised.[18] Given the imprecise and indiscriminate use that is often made of the term, it is worth recalling what the psychoanalytic concept of identification actually involves. In its original Freudian use identification is 'the original form of emotional tie with an object'.[19] Identification gives consistency to the subject by allowing it to assimilate certain attributes of its object (which is typically another person).[20] This process is central to Freud, since he comes to regard it as 'the operation… whereby the human subject is constituted'.[21] Jacques Lacan adopts a similar perspective, suggesting that identification is 'the transformation that takes place in the subject when he assumes an image'.[22] For Lacan, too, identification is a condition for the emergence of the subject although, crucially, he sees it as a process that is impossible to complete. This opens up the possibility of a political application of the concept. Identification cannot provide us with a stable identity, and it is this inadequacy which necessitates the continued attempt to identify with socially available discursive positions.[23] In the case of New Labour, for example, we are repeatedly offered the opportunity to identify ourselves as members of hard-working families.[24] What is crucial here is not the fact of our actual family or work arrangements, but the political meaning that is ascribed to them. New Labour 'speaks' to us as members of hard-working families. In so doing, it offers us a set of positions from which to engage with its political project, the acceptance (or rejection) of which partially constitutes us as political subjects. This process is uneven and necessarily incomplete, for both theoretical reasons – in adopting an identity that is offered to us we are actually *transforming* its meaning – and political ones, since New Labour discourse presupposes a certain family form (married with children) as typical. But in practice it actually takes a relatively consistent form, since the practical availability of discourses is severely limited and the offer of a leader-centred identification tends, in any case, to serve an integrative function.

Identification can take a variety of forms, of course. Freud's own understanding of the tie that binds us to political leaders, for example, was focused upon our taking the leader as an idealised figure whose authority is then internalised as part of our own conscience or superego. This conception seems foreign to us today, since we live in cynical times in which the superego has long been 'unmasked'.[25] But this does not mean that identification itself has diminished, and I want to argue that the specific form that our identification with political leaders takes is analogous to the way in which we relate to celebrities (or 'stars', as they are referred to in most of the critical literature). As Richard Dyer puts it, 'Stars represent typical ways of behaving, feeling and thinking in contemporary society, ways that have been socially, culturally, historically constructed ... Stars are also embodiments of the social categories in which people are placed and through which they have to make sense of their lives, and indeed through which we make our lives'.[26]

In other words, celebrity offers us an image of what is 'typical', which it then helps to create by inviting us to identify with that image.[27] Celebrity arouses strong emotion by promising an intimate encounter with someone whose personality has been exposed to close public scrutiny. Yet it presupposes an absence of direct, personal reciprocity. The celebrity is primarily known through a mass media which ordinary people can access only indirectly. Even when s/he is famed for being an 'ordinary person', this ordinariness is premised upon the *extra*ordinariness of that fame. For example, the fact that Blair has 'taken the trouble to "really listen"' – as one *New Woman* interviewer put it – is noteworthy precisely because he is famous and so a little bit different from us.[28] By highlighting the extraordinariness of celebrity, 'we' are also speaking about the ordinariness of our own lives. Making claims about celebrities, including political leaders, settles us into our 'natural' place within society.[29]

While it is still relatively novel to interpret British political leaders in this light, the tendency of these leaders to stress their (extraordinary) ordinariness is not new. Harold Wilson tailored his appearance and the public projection of his personality so as to appear an 'ordinary chap'. He even starred in a TV programme in which he revisited his school and childhood homes in Huddersfield.[30] Subsequent party leaders and prime ministers have followed suit. Margaret Thatcher keenly projected the persona of an ordinary person,

> the tradesman's daughter, the person who talks of 'little' issues, housekeeping for example, expresses 'little' emotions, perpetually giving voice to the desires and anxieties of 'ordinary people', often to the point where she conveys the notion that she, like them, is not interested in politics, but is simply the woman we see bustling about with her handbag on her arm.[31]

'Kinnock the Movie', a 1987 Labour election broadcast, was an attempt to do the same – although the emphasis on the leader's impoverished background was ill-suited to the film's triumphalist tone. John Major, who rode to victory in the 1992 election on the back of a soapbox, also used his supposed 'ordinariness' to political ends. As one contemporary commentator put it: 'His very ordinariness is an asset. Traditionally, the British feel comfortable with extraordinary ordinary men and distrust flashy politicians ... He is trying to persuade everyone in Britain that there are no barriers to their achieving what they wish to achieve'.[32]

Most recently, Tony Blair has also played on his ordinariness, inadvertently reinforcing his celebrity status in the process: 'I never expected to be a celebrity and I'm actually very normal'.[33] Blair's accent, his use of the vernacular, and his willingness to be photographed in casual clothes or filmed with a mug of tea all help in the marketing of Blair's normality.[34]

Blair and family

Tony Blair is not projected as a charismatic leader but is treated as 'one of us', although the precise nature of that 'us' tends to vary according to the audience he is addressing.[35] He enjoys 'fish and chip suppers' when talking to *The Sun*, and 'pasta with sun-dried tomatoes' when writing for an Islington charity cookery book. He is the Tabloid Blair who likes the Beatles, REM, Simply Red 'and classics too', and the inhabitant of Radio 4's Desert Island who enjoys Bruce Springsteen, Free and Ezio on the one hand, and Debussy and Samuel Barber's 'Adagio for Strings' on the other.[36] Different aspects of the Blair personality are emphasised in accordance with the expected audience, so that we might identify with him or, at least, see that he is acting in accordance with contemporary ideas of how a leader should be.

Cherie Blair is also marketed in this way. She is a 'working mother' rather than a 'Superwoman', according to one early profile. In Tony Blair's own words 'she is not a First Lady' – a response to the *Mail* and other hostile (not to mention sexist) tabloids which sought to characterise 'Ms Cherie Booth, QC' as an 'excessively powerful' wife and career woman, who would use her husband's influence to advocate gay rights, race and equality tribunals and a human rights commission.[37] Cherie, as seen through Tony's eyes, is a modern woman with 'her own career and three kids to worry about'.[38] She may be a career woman, but she is also the 'Mum who does most of the housework.'[39]

This public presentation of the Blairs' family and household routines is a crucial part of rendering them 'ordinary'. Tony Blair describes himself as 'just another Dad' and has often spoken of his love for Cherie.[40] The projection of the Blairs as an ordinary family provides us with an image through which we can identify with them as being 'like us'. More importantly, it also allows us to register and reaffirm certain ideas about the 'ordinariness' of a specific form of family life: married working parenthood.[41] The Blairs personify the New Labour project by offering us an image in which we can emerge as the political subjects to whom it speaks:

> As a dual earner career couple inhabiting No 10, the Blairs certainly have a strong symbolic appeal. They act as a reference point, a mirror to our own lives. We see them juggling work and life, pioneering new roles, wrestling for that elusive balance between work and life.[42]

The 'dual earning career couple' – or what is more frequently labelled the hard-working family – is naturalised as the ideal position from which to view New Labour discourse. Moreover, this description of the Blair family is not politically neutral because its meaning emerges in the context of a New Labour project that accords the family a central role. Elements of Blair's biography and personal style are repeatedly woven into the policy and ideological commitments he puts across.[43] Blair himself is a communitarian who emphasises the centrality of the family, calling it 'the essential bedrock of society'.[44]

The fact that Blair is a parent also enters into his rhetoric. At the launch of the 1997 Labour manifesto, for example, he chose to speak to his audience as a parent rather than just a political leader: 'I don't want second best for my kids and I don't want second best for yours'.[45] In the course of the same campaign, he also invoked his extended family in order to create a favourable contrast between himself and his Conservative opponents:

> My children make me think about the type of society we live in. I've been burgled, my mother-in-law's been mugged and had to give up work afterwards, my kids all go to state schools, so I think I'm probably more in touch than the average Conservative minister.[46]

The message was carefully chosen. Blair knows what the electorate wants, whereas the Conservatives are out of touch. He is ordinary and in touch. A family man. This is presented as the basis upon which he can be trusted.

Trust Tony

Political commentators were quick to pick up upon the important role that the Blair personality could play in legitimising New Labour politics. Dave Hill, writing in the *New Statesman* in September 1995, suggested that

> the credibility of the New Labour project depends heavily on Blair's ability to persuade voters to trust him personally, to believe that he personifies the principles he preaches, that there is something in the values he promotes in which they can share and in which they can profit, too. Trusting Tony Blair is the first prerequisite of trusting in the worth of his New Britain.[47]

It would be possible, I suppose, to specify grand sociological reasons as to why trust became a central political theme. Some fashionable strands of centre- and centre-left thinking have argued that the left-right ideological divide is in terminal decline, and that this process runs in parallel to the dealignment of politics from its traditional class basis. The old guarantees – class and socialism – no longer hold sway, and as a result it is becoming increasingly vital to command the electorate's trust.[48] Yet this particular type of analysis, which conflates two separate and contestable trends, is already politically loaded, and it is no accident that many of its principle exponents have also ended up as Blair's dinner guests.

A more prosaic, but ultimately more convincing, interpretation of New Labour's emphasis on trust would look at more immediate political concerns. 'Trust' was developed as an antidote to the perceived 'sleaze' of Major's Conservative party. With the Conservatives suffering a damaging series of sexual and financial scandals throughout the mid-1990s, and the party's credibility irreparably damaged by the ERM fiasco of September 1992, Labour sought to present itself as a safe alternative.

For the self-styled modernisers who now controlled the Labour Party, this meant far more than simply avoiding corruption. 'Trust' was also a palliative to Labour's bitter disappointment at defeat in the 1992 General Election. The modernisers blamed that calamity on the party's lack of credibility on the key issue of taxation, and its failure to address the aspirations of hard-working middle-class families.[49] When Tony Blair launched the 1997 Labour manifesto as a 'bond of trust', which he then sought to personalise as 'MY bond of trust with the people of Britain', this was accompanied by a pledge not to raise taxes and a carefully tailored appeal to 'ordinary' families.[50] In this way, the meaning of trust was closely articulated to the projection of a family-man image.[51]

Blair the individual was, and is, first and foremost Blair the family man. Part of his apparent trustworthiness stems from this fact: he claims to understand at first hand the problems that families face so he can be trusted to look after their interests. Identification is the crucial mechanism by which this bond is secured, since the continuation of an affective tie between Blair and 'the people' is the bedrock upon which trust is built. But this also renders Blair susceptible to attacks on this very stock of trust: the image of his (extraordinary) ordinariness, and the centrality of his family to his public persona. The Cheriegate scandal represents one such attack upon Blair's image, as well as dramatising the extent to which trust and the family have become central to it.

The Cheriegate scandal: trust, sleaze and spin

New Labour is not simply 'what Tony Blair does', but the image and perceived legitimacy of his leadership do play a central role in the advancement of its political project. As a result, the Government is permanently at risk from 'decapitation strikes' levelled at Blair, his family and his spin-machine.[52] Scandal offers Labour's opponents – principally the media – a political opportunity to undermine Blair. It is an opportunity to challenge the 'symbolic power in which reputation and trust are at stake.'[53] Whereas ideological struggle takes years of effort and investment, scandal can envelop a leader-centred party very quickly. This vulnerability is particularly acute when trust is invested in a leader's personality, as is the case with Blair, since personal reputation tends to be a non-renewable resource.[54]

Scandal itself is renewable, however, and this was clearly demonstrated in the way that Cheriegate became an occasion for the recollection of past misdemeanours – the Ecclestone affair, Peter Mandelson's resignation (twice), and the shaming of Geoffrey Robinson, Keith Vaz, and others. This concatenation of previous New Labour scandals was recalled in several newspaper articles, as well as on television reports. The reactivation of these past scandals framed the reception of Cheriegate which, in turn, was the context for their reiteration in the first place. As topics of public debate once more, the old scandals served as elements through which the meaning of Cheriegate could emerge. The 'murky £1 million donation from Formula One tycoon Bernie Ecclestone' was offered as proof that 'Labour has lined its coffers with cash from dodgy businessmen', while the resignations of Peter Mandelson and Stephen Byers were recalled to draw attention to the Government's 'obsession with spin'.[55] These were the 'hard facts' to which the tendentious claims of Cheriegate could be tethered. It didn't matter if those claims turned out to be true or false, since the articulation with elements of past scandal secured the same effect: to reinforce the perception of 'sleaze', which came to function as a nodal point organising the Cheriegate scandal. Where the substantive discoveries of Cheriegate proved lacking, the elements of past scandals were able to give meaning to the signifier 'sleaze'.

The Cheriegate case would appear to provide abundant evidence that the 'sleaze' label has infected New Labour's prestige. For example, a YouGov poll on 8 December revealed that 58% of people thought Labour should not be trusted, and that Tony Blair was considered the least trustworthy of the main political leaders. The whole story is not quite so simple, however, and we should also be sensitive to how this statistic was used to reproduce a scandal effect. Labour's media critics seized upon the YouGov poll and argued that 'it is now Labour that is seen by voters as the party of sleaze'.[56] As a result, this poll and others like it were themselves used to construct the sense of 'sleaze' and give legitimacy to the scandal narrative. They were reported as the true feelings of the people, without acknowledging the context of misinformation in which these public perceptions emerged. The polls also reinforced an emphasis on trust as *the* criteria upon which political leadership should now be judged.

The scandal effect was produced by reiteration. It took the form of a complex and seductive 'evidence game', spun into a self-reinforcing web of truth claims.[57] Even as the central accusations levelled at the Blairs remained unproven, the appearance of scandal that they generated – and the spectre of sleaze that emerged alongside it – was consistently *presupposed* as the basis upon which new claims were mounted. Many of the *Mail's* tendentious claims turned out to be untrue, but this did not disturb the unfolding of the story. As one correspondent to the BBC website put it: 'The matter isn't closed until she apologises to the public. I don't have a problem with her actions, she did nothing wrong legally, I just find it disgusting that the constant lies that have come out of Downing Street are considered acceptable by large amounts of people.'[58] He didn't believe the stories about Cherie, yet still found the whole situation scandalous.

Other correspondents to the BBC also saw little sign of wrongdoing, but were prepared for the media to keep digging until they found some! Effectively, they experienced the scandal cynically: 'I know very well that some of these stories are untrue, but this is still a scandal'.[59] Particular allegations about the Blairs' conduct were taken as evidence of generalised sleaziness and this, in turn, became the focus of much of the reporting and commentary on the Cheriegate affair. 'What is at issue here isn't Mrs Blair's judgment or lack of it but a cynical and continuing abuse of truth at the very heart of government that is corrupting public life', opined the *Daily Mail*.[60] The issue of Mrs Blair's judgment was recast as an issue of Mr Blair's judgement, which the *Mail* then sought to interpret as a question of 'the way this country is governed.'[61] This sounded like hyperbole to many correspondents to the BBC, who complained of 'a vitriolic campaign over nothing'. But the *Mail* and *Mirror* generally sought to pre-empt such criticisms: 'If Number 10 can't tell the truth over this, can they be trusted over anything?'.[62] In this way, they attempted to rework the triviality of the Cheriegate accusations into a marker of the government's dishonesty.

An emphasis on honesty meant that the issues of 'trust' and 'sleaze' were rearticulated in the light of the politics of spin. According to the *Daily Mail*, Cheriegate was 'the scandal of a mendacious No 10 Press machine and the issues of truth, trust and accountability'.[63] Stories in several newspapers also sought to envelop Alastair Campbell, the Prime Minister's director of communications, in the scandal.[64] Yet, as *The Guardian* pointed out, the Cheriegate scandal was in fact the product of successful spinning by the Blairs' media opponents. It was also a fairly monumental failure of spin on behalf of the Number 10 media machine, which not only failed in its attempts to bury the story, but inadvertently escalated it into a full-blown scandal by issuing a series of misleading and contradictory statements.[65]

The correspondence to the BBC website on this issue was remarkably sensitive to the presence of spin on all sides. Questions about the Blairs' honesty emerged as the central theme, but the media was also in the spotlight. Not surprisingly, responses to Cheriegate varied widely. A number of correspondents *did* conclude that the real issue was 'the probity and honesty of statements coming out of Downing Street', and that 'spin before truth seems to be the government's answer to any problem'. But several others weighed up Cherie Blair's credibility against that of the *Mail on Sunday* and found the newspaper wanting. Some correspondents generalised this point and attacked the 'gutter' press in general. More frequently, though, the media's critics sought to question the reporting of what seemed 'a non story, even to those of us who find Cherie Blair rather irritating'. As this last response shows, not all correspondents saw the matter in polarised terms. The response to Cheriegate was typically contradictory and 'dilemmatic', with many correspondents willing to find fault on all sides: 'There are three types of people in life you should never trust – politicians, lawyers and journalists.'[66]

In summary, the Cheriegate scandal reaffirmed the centrality of 'trust' to New Labour politics and its contestation in terms of both 'sleaze' and 'spin' claims. As I have shown, these claims were debated in terms of institutions, including the Downing Street press office and the media. But these institutions were not the key discursive terrain upon which the scandal was contested. For the most part, in fact, the meaning of 'trust' was debated in relation to the persona of Cherie Blair and, by extension, encompassed the Blair family image as a whole.

Cherie Blair: power-crazed celebrity or ordinary working mother?

The Cheriegate scandal concentrated a series of personalised attacks on Cherie Booth, with a view to undermining her husband. It is briefly worth recalling the context in which these attacks took place. The right-wing media has consistently presented Cherie as 'a highly political and public spouse,' deploring both her left-of-Tony past and her career as a QC 'profiteering' from the Human Rights Act.[67] These attacks became more sustained throughout 2002, with a combination of state occasions and Cherie's own occasional gaffes (an outburst on Palestine, the Queen Mother's funeral, the Golden Jubilee) taken as opportunities to scrutinise her role. The *Mail* and some of the Murdoch papers dubbed her Queen Cherie, condemning the very celebrity status that they had helped to confer with reports of her 'gracing the pages of *Hello!* magazine, alongside the likes of Posh Spice, in a push-up bra and a burgundy satin outfit worthy of a movie star.'[68] An unfavourable contrast was developed between the newly glamorous Cherie, and the figure who appeared on television news bulletins in May 1997 'wearing a generous helping of yesterday's make-up around her eyes and a nylon nightdress down to her knees'. Whereas this earlier persona had shown that 'the Blairs were real people just like us', the new celebrity Cherie was said to be 'arrogant'. Interestingly, celebrity and power were closely connected in this narrative of Cherie's increasingly exuberant role. Cherie emerged as 'the Queen of Downing Street, both a celebrity and a woman with perhaps more influence at the centre of power than any Prime Minister's wife (or husband) in history'.[69]

Unsurprisingly, the same perception of Cherie-the-celebrity was advanced during the Cheriegate scandal, where it was used to reinforce the contrast with the congenial figure of Cherie-the-working-mother: 'The idea that Mrs Blair thinks she's like other working mums shows how much celebrity and fame have corrupted her … We liked her ordinariness… And then she got fame and celebrity… it corrupted her. Cherie Blair is no longer ordinary… She's high-handed, arrogant and demanding.'[70] In this definition of celebrity, it was the *extra*ordinariness of Cherie that was stressed. But this wasn't an extraordinary ordinariness, inviting us to reflect upon and construct our own normality in the mirror of Cherie's banal everydayness. Rather, the tabloid media's celebrity spouse was presented as power-hungry and greedy. Wittingly or otherwise, these newspapers personified the dynamics of today's personalised political leadership in the figure of Cherie Blair. The effect was produced by a characteristically ideological reversal. Cherie's celebrity is predicated upon contemporary leadership's personalisation of power, but it was presented as a symptom of her desire for power.

This contest over the meaning of Cherie's celebrity status fed into a wider attack upon the Blair family as a source of the Prime Minister's legitimacy. As with Hilary Clinton in the US, Cherie was often presented as the power behind the throne. 'The woman who played a backseat role in Tony Blair's early political career now relishes her power over both her husband and the party', in the words of *Mail* columnist Linda Lee-Potter.[71] Throughout the Cheriegate scandal, this same logic was extended to the relation between Cherie and her 'intimate' adviser Carole Caplin: 'So influential is [Caplin] now and so closely does Mrs Blair seem to follow her advice that some New Labour disbelievers have nicknamed her "Cherie's Rasputin"'.[72] The story was, in fact, a rehash of an article that the *Mail* had published in May 2002, which began: 'Former soft porn model, ex-member of an insidious cult, how has this woman cast such an extraordinary spell over Mrs Blair?' In both cases, Cherie was presented as the power behind Tony Blair, and Carole Caplin as the power behind Cherie. The condensation of these two stories served to reinforce the *Mail's* master-narrative, which stressed the undemocratic and unaccountable nature of Cherie's influence: 'It is only in dictatorships and third world autocracies that the leader's wife gets to influence policy or poke her nose into court cases. It is squalid and humiliating that it is happening here.'[73]

This narrative of Cherie's unaccountable power was bound up with another, seemingly opposite story of Cherie's susceptibility to dangerous influences. For example, the *Sunday Mirror* of 8 December led with the news that Caplin's partner Peter Foster had planned to embroil the Blairs in a diet pill scam. Other articles focused on Carole Chaplin's purported influence in steering Cherie towards New Age mysticism: 'Carole could make Cherie do anything. She seemed to have some kind of power over her.'[74] Here, we find an instance of what

Jacqueline Rose has called celebrity's 'in-mixing of contraries,' in which Cherie figures as *both* domineering wife *and* weakest link.[75] As Polly Toynbee put it: 'the Cherie iconography is a rich tapestry of images – all of them nasty. She is the leftist harpy nagging her husband on policy, a Lady Macbeth avaricious for wealth and power or else the ditzy Catholic fruitcake dizzy on new age crystals and incense.'[76]

How are we to interpret these contrary images? In the first place, the combined effect of such stereotypical representations was to undermine Cherie's authenticity and thereby erode the grip of her celebrity status. 'Authenticity', as Richard Dyer reminds us, 'is both a quality necessary to the star phenomenon to make it work, and also the quality that guarantees the authenticity of the other particular values a star embodies.'[77] They were also clearly used to discredit the Prime Minister himself, as the intimation of contact between Caplin and Cherie was invoked to attack Tony Blair's judgement: 'Ms Caplin is said to be a regular guest at Chequers. For the Prime Minster to consort with such a person calls his own judgment into question.'[78] It is worth noting that the Prime Minister's judgement was thereby opened to question on the basis of a shared household space, rather than in relation to any political decision. The condition for the plausibility of this claim is that Blair's personality has become politically contested: the personal is political, as the anti-feminist *Mail* ironically reminded us. Finally, and most importantly, the multiple (and contrasting) stereotypes of Cherie were used to challenge the authenticity of the Blair family image as a whole: 'The trouble for the Blairs is the dissonance with the projection of them as a normal, wholesome, middle-class family who just happen to be living at Number 10, an image that has been hugely useful to the Prime Minister.'[79] Tabloid attacks on the Blairs – in particular, those emanating from the *Mail* – explicitly condemned her intrusion upon the public sphere, which remains a gendered terrain. Cherie was compared unfavourably with Norma Major and Audrey Callaghan, consorts who 'led private lives'.[80] At the same time, the same papers used Cherie's apparent transgression of the old public/private divide as a justification for their intrusion into her personal affairs. By becoming a public figure, they argued, she had abdicated her right to privacy.

The newspapers didn't have it all their own way, however, and Cherie eventually told her side of the story in an emotional television address on 11 December 2002. The crux of her statement sought to directly counter the Queen Cherie charge, and sought to reaffirm her status as an ordinary working mother:

> I'm the wife of the Prime Minister, I have an interesting job and a wonderful family, but I also know I am not Superwoman.
> The reality of my daily life is that I'm juggling a lot of balls in the air. Some of you must experience that.

> Trying to be a good wife and mother, trying to be the Prime Ministerial consort at home and abroad and being a barrister, a charity worker, and sometimes some of the balls get dropped.[81]

Cherie presented herself as a 'working mother' rather than a 'superwoman' – strikingly, the same terms that had been used to disavow the Hilary Clinton analogy in 1996. She appealed over the heads of the tabloid media to working mothers themselves. 'Some of you,' she said, experience a reality similar to 'my daily life.'

The phrasing obviously struck a cord with some working mothers: 'I suppose it makes more ordinary working mothers feel better about the difficulties they have juggling careers and family: if Cherie's fallible then there's hope for us all,' as one civil servant and mother told the next day's *Guardian*. Other respondents to the same *vox pop* even claimed that the affair had enhanced Cherie's reputation. 'I didn't admire her before the statement, but I admire her more now', one working mother commented, while another spoke of how 'She seems so much more human to me'.[82]

Some of the correspondence to the BBC website also suggests that the Blairs' reputation was enhanced by the affair, with approval of their 'great integrity and good family values in the face of constant public scrutiny and media intrusion'. Other correspondents also praised the Blair family's 'high level of integrity', and affirmed that 'Tony Blair and his wife are hardworking modern people'. The media's intrusion was rationalised in terms of its inability to cope with a 'relatively normal type of family' in No 10. It is a moot point whether or not these responses were and more representative than the claims made by others who saw her as 'arrogant' and 'very different to any working mums that we know because she's got all the extra help.' A 'snap' opinion poll conducted by ICM for *The Guardian* straight after Cherie's emotional statement found respondents to be fairly evenly split between those who were sympathetic to Cherie Blair (34%), those unsatisfied with her explanation (35%), and those who didn't express an opinion (31%).[83] But what is clear, from both an analysis of newspaper coverage of the affair and an exploratory study of responses to it, is that the integrity of the Blair family was a central theme during the Cheriegate scandal. The dispute dramatised and highlighted the proximity between today's political leadership and celebrity, and showed this to be closely articulated to perceptions of the 'ordinary' family.

Conclusion

This article has argued that the Blair leadership can fruitfully be interpreted in the light of celebrity, trust and the family. The presidentialisation of British politics has blurred the boundary between public and private. As a result, the Blair personality and family image have become important discursive terrains upon which to dispute the trustworthiness of his Government. Their centrality has been reinforced by Labour's own political marketing, which presented Blair as the personification of New Labour, the embodiment of its values and the source of its trustworthiness. Identification is a crucial aspect of this, since it supplies the affective ties around which trust can be built. Moreover, the type of identification appropriate to contemporary political leadership is not based upon charisma or idealisation (as Weber and Freud thought) but is focused on extraordinary-ordinariness – a modality more commonly associated with celebrity. Blair is ordinary. He has a two-income family, and so understands the problems faced by working parents. As this is supposed to be an *extra*ordinary situation for a Prime Minister, we are invited to focus upon his banal acts with a curiosity which we would not turn to our own everyday lives. The Blairs' ordinariness presents us with an opportunity to reflect upon our own ordinariness. It holds up a mirror through which we can transform ourselves into New Labour subjects. But in the Blair-centred world of New Labour politics, the party's prestige is highly susceptible to 'decapitation strikes' upon the leadership. Tony Blair's trustworthiness was attacked during the Cherigate scandal via the perceived follies of his wife, and his family man image was compromised by the presence of Cherie's 'weirdo pals.' Both the structure of the Cheriegate scandal, and the attacks in response to it, reveal the importance and the centrality of the themes of trust and the family to any understanding of the Blair presidency.

Notes

1. Linda Colley, 'That's no way to treat a first lady', *Guardian*, 18 December 2002.
2. Trevor Kavanagh, 'It's time to ditch those weirdo pals', *Sun* 6 December 2002.
3. Paul Harris, 'Weird World of Cherie', *Daily Mail*, 3 December 2002.
4. Ibid; Natalie Clarke and Paul Bracchi, 'Carole's secret past', *Daily Mail*, 19 December 2002.
5. Gordon Rayner and Richard Shears, 'Cherie, a Crook, and the Proof No 10 Lied', *Daily Mail*, 5 December 2002, p1.
6. Timothy Bewes reaches a similar conclusion regarding the cash-for-contracts scandal of summer 1998: 'The most immediate conclusion to draw from the episode was that there was nothing *substantially* insidious about New Labour. This was no controversy over policy, for example, but rather a mood, a perception – an *image*. It is not wrongdoing, any longer, but the *appearance* of wrongdoing that has become impeachable.' See his 'Truth and appearance in politics' in Tim Bewes and Jeremy Gilbert (eds), *Cultural capitalism: politics after New Labour*, Lawrence and Wishart, London 2000, p161.
7. Martin Smith and Andrew Chapman, 'Blair's "Used Fraudster to Buy Flats"', *Mail on Sunday*, 1 December 2002, p1.
8. Cherie Blair, 'I just wanted to protect my family', *Guardian*, 11 December 2002.
9. 'Sense and Perspective', *The Times*, 11 December 2002.
10. Andrew Rawnsley, 'The Fire Next Time for New Labour', *Observer*, 15 December 2002.

11. Polly Toynbee, 'They can't beat the man, so they spit venom at his wife', *Guardian*, 12 December.
12. Lesley Ann Jones, 'My kids stop me getting too big-headed: Tony Blair', *News of the World*, 29 Oct 1995.
13. P. David Marshall, *Celebrity and Power*, University of Minnesota Press, Minneapolis 1997, p19.
14. There are actually at least three literatures on political leadership: institutional role (office of the prime minister), which overlaps with writings on the British constitution; political communications and marketing, which overlaps with writing on voting behaviour; and social and moral capital.
15. Michael Foley is the leading exponent of this view. See his *The British Presidency*, Manchester University Press, Manchester 2000.
16. Foley, op cit, p258. It should be noted that the presidentialisation thesis is not individualist, but is cast in terms of structural and political changes – most notably, the role of the mass media and contemporary news values.
17. Ibid, p.177.
18. This is an adaptation of the psychoanalytic definition of identification offered in J. Laplanche and J.B. Pontalis, *The Language of Psychoanalysis*, Karnac, London 1967, p206.
19. Sigmund Freud, 'Group Psychology and the analysis of the ego', in *Civilisation, Society and Religion. Pelican Freud Library vol. 12*, Penguin, Harmondsworth 1985, pp134-140. In fact, Freud distinguishes three modes of identification: it is also the regressive substitute for an abandoned object-choice, and a perception that another person shares a common trait with oneself, even though that person is not one's sexual object.
20. For Freud, an object is typically a love-object: 'the thing in respect of which and through which the instinct seeks to attain its aim', Laplanche and Pontalis, op cit, p273.
21. Laplanche and Pontsalis, op cit, p206.
22. Jacques Lacan, *Écrits*, Tavistock, London 1977, p2.
23. Yannis Stavrakakis, *Lacan and the Political*, Routledge, London 1999, p36.
24. See my 'New Labour's politics of the hard-working family' in David Howarth and Jacob Torfing, *Discourse Theory and European Politics*, forthcoming.
25. Max Horkheimer, cited Michael Billig, *Talking of the Royal Family*, Routledge, London 1998, p.88. 'The father may still possess a super-ego, but the child has long unmasked it'.
26. Richard Dyer, *Heavenly Bodies*, Macmillan, Basingstoke 1987, p18.
27. Although, if we take seriously a commitment to understanding celebrity as a discursive terrain, then the 'audience' must also be conceived of as agents conferring this status upon a person: 'The celebrity's power is derived from the collective configuration of its meaning; in other words, the audience is central in sustaining the power of any celebrity sign.' Marshall, op cit, p65.
28. 'Yes…Yes…Yes, Prime Minister', *New Woman*, 6 April 2000.
29. Michael Billig, *Talking of the Royal Family*, Routledge, London 1998, p23. Billig refers to this as 'double-declaiming'.
30. Martin Rosenbaum, *From Soapbox to Soundbite*, Macmillan, Basingstoke 1997, p193.
31. John Gaffney, *The Language of Political Leadership in Contemporary Britain*, Macmillan, Basingstoke 1991, p5.
32. Bruce Anderson, cited in Michael Foley, *The British Presidency*, Manchester UP, Manchester 2000, p153.
33. *New Woman*, op cit.
34. See Norman Fairclough, *New Labour, New Language?*, Routledge, London 2000, pp97-105 and Alan Finlayson, *Making Sense of New Labour*, Lawrence and Wishart, London 2003, pp51-58.

35. Finlayson, op cit, p54.
36. John Rentoul, *Tony Blair*, Warner, London 2001, p301; Sue Evison, 'Tony Blair opens his heart to *The Sun*', *Sun*, 27 February 1997; Anne Karpf, 'Blair the blushing man of integrity elbowed out by Blair the campaigning politician,' *Guardian*, 25 November 1996.
37. Niall Ferguson, 'Will Cherie be Britain's Hillary?', *Daily Mail*, 4 February 1996.
38. Carole Aye Maung, 'The Real Cherie Blair', *Daily Mirror*, 9 September 1996; Piers Morgan, 'Tony Blair: his first interview as Prime Minister,' *Daily Mirror*, 29 July 1997.
39. Evison, ibid.
40. Jones, op cit; Evison, op cit.
41. Billig, op cit, p86.
42. Helen Wilkinson, 'Time to Deliver on the Family', *Independent*, 21 November 1999.
43. Finlayson, op cit, pp51-2.
44. Lynda Lee-Potter, 'I am an emotional person: interview with Tony Blair', *Daily Mail*, 17 April 1998.
45. Kevin Maguire and Will Woodward, 'Trust me to make it better: Tony Blair launches Labour's election manifesto', *Daily Mirror*, 4 April 1997.
46. Tony Blair, 29 April 1997; Rentoul, op cit, pp257-9.
47. Dave Hill, 'Action Man', pp.24-8, *New Statesman*, 29 September 1995.
48. Anthony Giddens, *Beyond Left and Right*, Polity, Cambridge 1994, pp92-97 sees 'reflexive modernisation' as leading to a new 'life politics' in which 'active trust' plays a central role.
49. Philip Gould, *The Unfinished Revolution*, Little, Brown, London 1998, p158 and *passim*.
50. Trevor Kavanagh, 'My Bond with Britain: You can trust me Blair tells voters', *Sun*, 4 April 1997; Blair, 'We will govern as New Labour. That is my bond of trust with you', *Sun*, 18 Mar 1997.
51. Articulation is a political practice of linking together elements of a discursive formation such that their identity is modified in the process. See Ernesto Laclau and Chantal Mouffe, *Hegemony and Socialist Strategy*, Verso, London 1985, pp105-114.
52. Foley, p198: 'The public projection and private protectiveness of a leader-centred party and government carried concomitant risks of decapitation strikes through the development of a critical dimension related to the alleged abuses and excesses of media manipulation.'
53. John B. Thompson, *Political Scandal*, Polity, Cambridge 2000, p245.
54. Ibid, pp252-3.
55. 'The lies that could topple New Labour', *Daily Mirror*, 9 December 2002.
56. Ian Gallagher, 'Cherie to Back Guru in Public', *Mail on Sunday*, 8 December 2002, p1.
57. I borrow the term 'evidence game' rather loosely from Anna Marie Smith, *New Right Discourse on Race and Sexuality*, Cambridge University Press, Cambridge 1994, pp192-196.
58. This and other BBC website quotations are all sourced from 'Talking Point', http://news.bbc.co.uk/1/hi/talking_point/2555905.stm, accessed 17 December 2002. This site is more like a large *vox pop* than a chat room. The quotations are interpreted as indicative of how public respondents understand Cheriegate, and aim to highlight some of the 'common sense' assumptions made. They are *not* taken to be representative of public opinion as a whole.
59. Slavoj Zizek interprets this type of cynicism as the typical mode of operation for contemporary ideology, in *The Sublime Object of Ideology*, Verso, London 1989, p33.
60. 'Opportunities the Tories are Wasting', *Daily Mail*, 7 December 2002.
61. 'A Free Press', *Daily Mail*, 12 December 2002; 'All we want is honesty from No 10', *Mirror*, 13 December 2002.

62. David Hughes and Gordon Rayner, 'They still can't tell the truth', *Daily Mail*, 6 December 2002, p1.
63. 'Opportunities the Tories are Wasting', *Daily Mail*, 7 December 2002.
64. Gordon Rayner et al., 'The truth, the whole truth, and anything but the truth', *Daily Mail*, 10 December 2002.
65. Nicholas Watt, 'How a little local difficulty began to spin out of control', *Guardian*, 6 December 2002; 'A problem that became a fiasco', *Observer*, 15 December 2002.
66. See Billig et al, 1988.
67. Margaret Cook, 'Superwoman?', *Daily Mail*, 12 December 2002.
68. Linda MacDougall, 'How Cherie lost the plot', *Sunday Times*, 23 June 2002. See also: 'Cherie is often out on the town, and loves to be pictured with celebrities', and Stephen Glover, 'Has Cherie become a serious liability?', *Daily Mail*, 19 June 2002.
69. Geoffrey Levy, 'Queen Cherie', *Daily Mail*, 11 May 2002.
70. Carole Malone, 'Arrogance with a Cherie on top', *Daily Mirror*, 15 December 2002.
71. Linda Lee-Potter, 'How gullible Cherie is the power behind Tony's throne', *Daily Mail*, 4 December 2002.
72. Harris, op cit.
73. Peter Hitchens, 'Shed no tears please, she's tougher than a Scouse docker', *Daily Mail*, 15 December 2002. In psychoanalysis, condensation occurs when a single term comes to represent several associative chains at whose point of intersection it is located. Cf Laplanche and Pontalis, op cit, pp82-3.
74. Martin Smith, 'Carole could make Cherie do anything', *Mail on Sunday*, 8 December 2002.
75. Jacqueline Rose, 'The Cult of Celebrity', *London Review of Books*, vol. 20 No. 16, 20 August 1998.
76. Polly Toynbee, 'They can't beat the man, so they spit venom at his wife', *Guardian*, 12 December.
77. Richard Dyer, '*A Star is Born* and the Construction of Authenticity', in C Gledhill, ed. *Stardom: Industry of Desire*, Routledge, London 1991, p133.
78. Melanie Phillips, 'Private? No, this is a very public affair', *Daily Mail*, 9 December 2002.
79. Andrew Rawnsley, 'Cherie Blair's dangerous liaisons', *Observer*, 8 December 2002.
80. Cook, op cit.
81. Cherie Blair, op cit.
82. Hadley Freeman et al, 'Did Cherie win your sympathy?', *Guardian*, 12 December 2002.
83. Alan Travis, 'Voters divided over Mrs Blair's version of events', *Guardian*, 13 December 2002.

The especially remarkable
Celebrity and social mobility in Reality TV

Anita Biressi and Heather Nunn

This article examines the promotion of the 'ordinary' person as a celebrity within a modern democratic social realm. It argues that the transformation of media culture through new forms such as Reality TV in Britain has increasingly allowed for the rise to celebrity status of those who have neither cultural capital nor elite roles in the public sphere. It explores how these subjects become iconic through their newly found social mobility.

Introduction: celebrity in the modern social realm

With New Labour's inception in 1997, arts and entertainment celebrities gained prominence as exemplars of a new meritocratic and essentially *modern* democratic social realm.[1] The administration at Number 10 Downing Street actively sought the endorsement of musicians, actors and movie stars in its attempts to deploy a new, more inclusive and populist lexicon as part of its electoral address and managerial style. As a consequence, it was those who had succeeded in entertainment, rather than, say, industry or finance, who were often held up as exemplary figures 'close to' New Labour. Such entertainers and sports people, some originally from very disadvantaged social backgrounds, came to the fore as people of influence and social standing.

In the same cultural moment, the notable success of new TV forms – docusoaps such as *The Cruise* and hybrid 'reality' shows such as *Big Brother* and later *Pop Idol* – enabled the transformation of the terrain of media culture which, in turn, showcased ordinary people as potential media stars.[2] The modern social realm was, it seems, further expanded to accommodate a new band of celebrities, of ordinary people rendered remarkable through their encounter with new hybrid media forms and by their imbrication with the complex processes of identification and voyeurism that made them household names. These new media stars appeared to be able to 'make it big', to not only become wealthy but, more importantly, to sustain a transformation into celebrity stardom without overtly drawing on education, entrepreneurial skills or even any obvious talent.

Reality television's development of new iconic personas and their facilitation into a media-driven social mobility was, of course, partly anticipated by longer-established media narratives of class mobility. Biographies and news coverage of celebrity British footballers, pop performers, comedians and film stars have been central to the mythologisation of working-class social mobility in media culture. So too, narratives of football pools wins, bullion heists and lottery jackpots have long provided fantasy avenues of escape that were independent of the cultural capital gained through education, birth, entry into the professions or even talent (aside from the talent, that is, to entertain).[3]

The successful launch of the television drama series *Footballers' Wives* is a good example of a public fascination with the transformation of ordinary people into a new media-ocracy through fame, personal achievement and stunning affluence. The focus of the series, which has its roots in tabloid women's magazines such as *Hello!* and *OK*, did not dwell on the skills of players but on the fame and fortune of the newly affluent and media-savvy footballer and his wife as celebrities.[4] The depiction of Victoria and David Beckham and their family life as 'popular royals' (resident in 'Beckingham Palace') was one clear influence on the programme. Their lives are exemplary too of a doubled agenda that famous working-class celebrities need to negotiate if they are to remain in favour. They must maintain the much-mythologised 'down-to-earth' values of working-class family culture and authenticity while fulfilling the expectations of glamour and overt consumption that sustain their public personas. They operate as an important counterpoint to those born into celebrity during a period when, for example, the public no longer feels obliged to look to the monarchy or other elite persons for role models of exemplary domesticity or overt consumption.[5]

The popular impact of these and other celebrities seems to reside precisely in their very disconnection from traditional structures of influence (inheritance, education, etc) together with their intimate connection with the media and the consumer lifestyle which the media privileges and foregrounds.[6] Although celebrities have been described by some media critics as a 'powerless elite'[7], they wield a form of power formerly unrecognised as such. Graeme Turner *et al* have argued, for example, that:

> ...the celebrity's ultimate power is to sell the commodity that is themselves. This fact has been thoroughly integrated into contemporary popular culture and the marketing of celebrity-as-commodity has been deployed as a major strategy in the commercial construction of social identity.[8]

In this context, the *accoutrements* and *appearance* of celebrity are paramount. Although the celebrity is a figure of consumption writ large they must also retain the individualism that marks them apart and renders them remarkable and commercially marketable. What might be called 'classed cross-dressing' becomes one overt and instantly recognisable expression of both their agency and their success. The sartorial and material signifiers of class transformation mark both working-class origins and the move away from them; the pleasurable and playful excess of financial escape from those origins and a rebuke or an offence against respectable 'taste'.[9] This move up is also problematised because class mobility is dependent on consumption or the unstable transformation of stardom. The dual dynamics of transformation and submerged 'real' classed identities that appear in many media representations of the socially mobile 'media-ocracy' are crucial. Focusing on the representation of social mobility and celebrity in Reality TV[10] we will consider the complex interdependence between class and performance, the freedom of taking on new identities and the notion of some hidden essence or 'true' working-class identity concealed beneath the 'glitz'.

Critical responses: disgust, democratisation and desire

> Reality TV is not the end of civilisation as we know it: it is civilisation as we know it. It is popular culture at its most popular, soap opera come to life.[11]

Current responses to Reality TV coalesce around several themes. One common strand is that of derision. This response is encapsulated in Germaine Greer's much cited quotation above. In her article on Reality TV, Greer jeers at the mass audience of these shows and predictably situates them within a 'dumbed down' tabloid TV arena in which, she claims, a mixture of banality, exhibitionism and character-play guarantee audience ratings and therefore their domination of the schedules.

In keeping with broader attacks on tabloid culture and of the 'feminisation' of factual programming, a number of cultural critics (often championing a lost cause which is implicitly 'high culture') decry those who produce, watch and perform for Reality TV's cameras. Here, the ethics of what is acceptably represented in the mass media is linked to broader debates about the decline of more privileged objective factual reportage and programming. In Britain, this debate is specifically linked to the role of television in an arena in which the public service ethos has been diminished. Objectivity, fact and debate are bandied about as lost values of a formerly intellectually curious journalistic age.[12]

The Reithian theme of self-improvement and a broadcasting service that strove to use television to take viewers outside their realm of immediate existence, to educate and inform, is lamented as a lost educative ideal in an increasingly commercially pressured media environment. Reality TV, it is claimed, replaces this intellectual adventure with the limited exhibitionist challenges of the game show or the emotional outpourings of confessional culture in which the biggest challenge is to get on with a small bunch of housemates/prisoners/competitors for a limited period.[13] With Reality TV the aim is not to take viewers outside of their own experience but to present them with a fully recognisable and familiar realm of the ordinary and the everyday. The ethic of self-improvement seems, for media sceptics, to be parodied; as those without the traditional markers of media role models are seen to succeed – if not in Reithian terms, then at least within the terms of the populist media.

The disdain for the entertainment-led audience is matched by distress about changes to televisual form and genre. Frequently, the documentary becomes the marker of quality filming based on rational investigation of historical or socio-cultural fact. The detached but committed observational gaze of the documentary maker of the past has, it is claimed, been replaced by a slow slide through the docu-soap of the 1990s to the current Reality TV show. An anxiety about the decline of documentary proper is often articulated to an anxiety about Reality TV's dependence on spectacle linked to a manipulative misuse of the camera. Here, the prominence of, for example, the 'close-up' is highlighted. This fear of the seductive image is captured in language that stresses the distraction of the viewer from rational viewing: ' we *cannot think straight*…if our *emotions* are being *jerked up and down* by …zoom lenses'.[14] Underlying this anxiety about 'easy' pleasure is recognition of the destabilisation of the distant and powerful documentary camera and the move towards televisual intimacy.

In contrast to the above criticism, others have celebrated this cultural phenomenon as part of the contemporary expansion and democratisation of public culture. It is argued that Reality TV's popular expression of social concerns and everyday events, conflicts and traumas within a highly managed environment signal the opening up of the public sphere to ordinary concerns and ordinary people who, if they are popular enough and lucky enough, can become famous. Where celebrities are already a prerequisite of the show – for example in the recent adaptations of survival shows for celebrity participants – the authenticity of the show is marked by the supposed provision of insights into the hidden 'real' aspect of celebrity personality. Phil Edgar-Jones, the executive producer of *Big Brother*, described the second *Celebrity Big Brother* as a stripping away of celebrity personas: 'With normal *Big Brother* we're making ordinary people extraordinary. With this, we're making famous people very, very ordinary'.[15] In short, Reality TV is celebrated as a democratisation of public culture and the deconstruction of the components of fame that partially constitute the celebrity media subject and the construction of social identity more broadly.

The process of constructing celebrity and stripping it away can be captured in John Langer's notion of 'the especially remarkable'.[16] In his analysis of tabloid culture, he highlights the prominence in current media culture of the 'other news': a form of cultural discourse intimately connected with gossip, story-telling and the scrutiny of the newly famous as well as those with a longer-held celebrity persona. Langer situates his celebrities within a co-dependent media context in which celebrity status is both ratified by media presence but also operates as a privileged authority in media culture. Celebrities have increasingly taken on the role as 'primary definers' of news. The very force of representation of the celebrity gives their actions and statements a kind of privileged authority in a world increasingly characterised as divided by those who have access to image-making and the rest.[17] This other news does not represent elite persons within the context of their institutional backdrop and does not primarily consider their role as power brokers or decision makers – but rather values their informal activities, public rituals of display and consumption, and their private lives.

This 'calculus of celebrity'[18], then, is flexible, and focuses not only on celebrities but those who have achieved possibly fleeting public attention through specific personal achievements.[19] For example, the 'ordinary' stars of Reality TV shows suddenly acquire massive media visibility but possess very little in the way of institutional power or control and, unless they obtain excellent PR management, they often have little experience in media spin. It could be suggested then that Reality TV both proves and extends the mythic belief that traditional versions of mobility and success, once closely associated with economic or social terms, are increasingly implicated in and subsidiary to the mass media processes of publicity. Langer suggests:

> On the one hand ordinary people are constructed as especially remarkable for what they do. How they breach expectations, their remarkableness, is lodged in the extraordinary acts they perform. This separates them from us, makes them different and transcendent; they start where we are but move beyond. On the other hand …The implication is that, although these people are assigned especially remarkable qualities based on what they do, such qualities and performances could just as easily be within our grasp. If those seemingly mundane occupations and enthusiasms … can become the springboard from which those ordinary people ascend into the realms of the especially remarkable, it could just as easily happen to us as well.[20]

The appeal of Reality TV lies partly in how seemingly unremarkable people are suddenly 'especially remarkable' and how that celebrity status is endorsed by the spectacle of their widespread public presence. For example, the UK series *Pop Idol UK*, which ran in the summer of 2002, screened countless auditions of would-be pop celebrities. The show attracted over 30 million viewers who watched and voted for those singers who would remain until the final contest between Gareth Gates and the ultimate winner Will Young.[21] These two contestants have both become chart-topping pop singers with massive media coverage.[22]

The 2002 spin-off *American Idol* warned potential contestants that their appearance on TV may be 'disparaging, defamatory, embarrassing or of an otherwise unfavourable nature which may expose you to public ridicule, humiliation or condemnation'.[23] Nonetheless its popularity with would-be idols and audiences alike ensured a second series in 2003. *American Idol 2* appeared on Fox TV and concurrently in the UK on ITV2 in March 2003. It followed the structure of the UK predecessor and the final 12 contestants were introduced to their audience through pre-recorded video cameos that emphasised their 'ordinariness', their small-town America homes and the support of their local schools, military barracks, church or family. These to-camera testimonies by family and friends and shots of the contestants feeding the ducks, visiting their old workplace at a hair salon or supermarket, or training with ordinary soldiers, located them as 'no-one particularly special', as 'regular' or 'all-American' young men and women. But, at the same time, the 'folks' that spoke of them and their singing skills, as a child amateur performer, in the Church choir, in a local bar, served to elevate their status. These subsidiary characters, like the live audience for whom the contestants then perform, function textually as a sign of public acclamation: 'the especially remarkable are seen (by us) to be seen by others in the public domain'.[24]

These short video narratives of personal triumph over ordinary obstacles and *over obscurity itself* anticipated their live stage performance singing before music industry judges and audience. The appearance in front of TV cameras before a voting TV audience was constructed consequently as the tangible reward for their accomplishments *per se* despite the lure of winning the competition. In such competitions, the ordinary masses of viewers who follow the course of the contestant's path to fame are crucial. They serve a similar role to the subsidiary characters present at the edges of the frame in TV camera or paparazzi shots of the star persona, for their presence 'watching, waiting, attending or serving' the ordinary celebrity endorses his or her status.[25] Furthermore, this identification with the 'especially remarkable' individual allows for the possibility of a sense of activity for the TV spectator, of a hand in the elevation of the ordinary person to celebrity status.

Correspondingly, Peter Balzagette, creative director of Endemol Entertainment UK, the creators of *Big Brother* in the UK, argued in the 2001 Huw Wheldon lecture to his media industry peers that Reality TV is 'diverse programming, and access to the airwaves for a more diverse spread of people'.[26] He declared that this democratisation, also signalled by the audience's ability to contribute to the elevation or elimination of the stars, goes hand in hand with a change in social attitudes about television and identification. He characterises this as a desire for 'emotional investment' latched onto the appeal of interactivity and audience participation. For Balzagette, audience figures clarify this desire to participate in and determine a programme's conclusion; a motivation which ensured that over the first two series of *Big Brother* around 34 million phone votes were cast for who should stay and who should go in the *Big Brother* house.[27]

This investment, articulated through constant media, especially tabloid press, coverage, is apparent and increasingly dominant in the most recent *Big Brother* production.[28] This third series which ran in the summer of 2002 followed the standard formula of isolating 12 voluntary participants in a house without media contact with the outside world for 64 days. These were gradually eliminated and ejected by telephone poll until the winner remained. In the final week of the programme, 8.5 million votes were cast, signalling for some media commentators that the series epitomised 'the model of participatory programming'.[29] The press measured the extent of its success by competing for exclusive interviews as the final four to emerge from the house were deluged with cash offers; the figures offered often dwarfed the £70,000 prize collected by the eventual winner, 22-year-old Kate Lawler.

But the issues we have raised about the seemingly unremarkable subject of Reality TV and their entry into the celebrity matrix are best exemplified by Jade Goody. Jade Goody, a 21 year old dental nurse from South London, fourth from last to be expelled from the house, received wildly fluctuating media coverage from the press whilst in the house and was the subject, halfway through the series, of vitriolic attacks from the tabloids. Goody was undoubtedly 'marked' negatively as working-class by her body, her voice and her supposed intellectual ignorance. She was loud, apparently uneducated, bibulous, excessive, overweight and getting fatter as the series progressed. The press revelled in quoting 'Jade-isms', the stupid things said by Goody in the course of the series. She displayed the bodily excesses that marked Roseanne Barr as a blatantly working-class woman but without the wisecracking humour that protected Barr from the worst misogynistic criticisms. Dominic Mohon, editor of the *Sun*'s showbiz column 'Bizarre', urged readers to evict Jade with the deeply misogynistic slogan, 'Vote out the pig'. He informed readers that 'Jade is one of the most hated women on British TV and life will be hard for her when she leaves the house'. She seemed to exemplify Annette Kuhn's observation that:

> Class is something beneath your clothes, under your skin, in your psyche, at the very core of your being. In the all-encompassing English class system, if you know you are in the 'wrong' class, you know that therefore you are a valueless person.[30]

However, tabloid attacks were upturned by positive viewer support for Goody resulting in tabloid battles for exclusive rights to her when she emerged from the house. Ironically, Rupert Murdoch's *Sun* and *News of the World* outbid rival tabloids and paid £500,000 for exclusive interviews with her. Since then Goody has been re-branded as a 'national treasure'.

Jade Goody's success fits the pattern highlighted for the 'especially remarkable' in that when the ordinary celebrity is prone to setbacks, these setbacks are played out before the public gaze. She won through only after a dialectic of ill-fortune and effort had been played out. And crucially her success was attributed to powers beyond her grasp or ken: she was subject to the inexplicable hand of fate, the power of the TV audience and the manipulations of the TV production crew. When she exited from the House she appeared dressed in a glamorous evening gown three sizes too small and was soon confronted by *Big Brother* host Davina McCall with a montage of clips revealing her excessive behaviour and her apparent stupidity. She was greeted by talk show comedian Graham Norton, who reclaimed her as a camp icon, the plump, giggly and dense dental nurse reminiscent of a 1950s *Carry On* film.

Subsequent media coverage focused on the re-education of Miss Goody. The TV programme *What Jade Did Next* (Channel 4, October 2002) followed her as she worked with a personal trainer, learned how to deal with the media, learned how to drive and was schooled in the very demanding work of public appearances. Her background with her single mother on a working-class social housing estate was contrasted with the opportunities on offer to her since her appearance on the reality show. She was a stark signifier of the possibility of self-transformation and social mobility in spite of class origins and limited social skills. Jade's narrative of desired transformation also reveals how class plays a central role in the production of femininity and the regulation of it. The escape which Jade articulates in *What Jade Did Next* reveals a knowledge on her part about the attainment of not just economic wealth but the cultural artefacts of taste and knowledge; of cultural capital. The possession of the 'right' car, of literacy, of designer clothes and private property are signifiers of social mobility hedged with the dangers of the disreputable: the trashy dress, the uninformed opinion, the too-loud laugh. In keeping with earlier fictional fantasies of achievement, Reality TV offered Jade Goody a way to exhibit incipient talent for performance, 'rough at the edges but with the potential for learning'.[31]

The vitriolic attacks on Jade and the manipulative techniques used on the participants of the third *Big Brother* generated popular debates about the ethical and moral conundrums spawned by some Reality TV programmes. For example, in this series the participants were frequently stimulated into exhibitionist or adversarial behaviour having been plied with vast quantities of alcohol which replaced former routine activities such as reading books, a pastime removed from the contestants. Games were devised to generate tensions between house members. Penalties involved the enforced separation of participants who had formed emotional ties and a fast-or-feast division in which the losing group were subjected to deprivation of food and basic facilities whilst the winners celebrated with plentiful food and other treats. The clear aim was to initiate volatile emotions: guilt, jealousy and paranoia ensued. Viewers were treated to simmering feuds, which resulted in one contestant, Sandy, escaping from the house not to return and another, Sunita, walking out. Sexual tension and jealousy were provoked and a number of cultural commentators were prompted to question the slippage towards exploitation illustrated by scenes such as a drunken Goody, filmed stripping naked amidst seemingly less impressionable fellow housemates.

Such displays yielded larger audiences and advertising revenues. The second instalment of the show (in the post-watershed slot 10-11.30pm) attracted an average of 9.4 million viewers: a 49% share of the audience and the channel's highest daily audience share in its nineteen-year history. These figures peaked on the final night at 9.9 million (the previous year had peaked at 8.8 million) according to unofficial figures. However, there were concerns that Reality TV was, in its search for innovation, increasingly fostering the brute forces of our psyche. The *Guardian* noted that, 'When it started, Big Brother had lofty pretensions to examine the company of strangers', but, it contended, 'social observation has yielded to darker impulses – to stir conflict, polarise and humiliate'.[32] This trajectory to disturb, provoke the base emotions and to humiliate contestants is one which celebrity aspirants need to negotiate with care.

Celebrity hybridity and packaged demotic culture

The address to the Reality TV audience varies depending on the format of the show. But across the board there is a shared assumption that the audience possesses the media-literate capabilities to judge the contestants/participants of the Reality TV show – even though the criteria of judgement are often un-formulated and unspoken. These criteria are grounded in vague notions of identification, appreciation and also crucially of dislike and disdain. Participants of *Big Brother* or *Pop Idol* or *The Club* (ITV2 2003) knowingly present themselves to a judgmental audience. Their task is one of interaction and the overt immersion in the competitive structure of the show. Selected on the basis of contradictory criteria, participants are often stereotypes of the diverse identities that populate contemporary media culture – lesbian or gay, black, heterosexual bachelor, twenty/thirty-something white 'Essex' girl or boy, stud, tart, shy loner. These types share (are presented as sharing) two features: an everyday commonality and a hunger/persistence for celebrity status. The winning formula for appearance on the Reality TV show appears to be a combination of the typecast, the banal and the exceptional.

Frequently, the participants are presented as classed subjects. Whilst the boundary between working class and lower middle class is now often blurred, the participants generally are presented as residing somewhere in this region: they are clerical workers, mechanics, bar keepers, service industry workers and so on. They are also frequently aspirant media celebrities. In many Reality TV shows there is a submerged narrative about escape across classed boundaries. Also the production and editing of the show reveals a level of unacknowledged cultural capital at play. The taste and disposition of the contestants is under scrutiny; their clothes, banal conversation, interactions with other contestants, ambitions, everyday activities as related to the audience are markers of their position within the class hierarchy. The importance here is to appear not *too* wealthy, *too* cultured or *too* tasteful. Yet, as with Jade Goody, to appear too trashy, too sexual, too uncultured can also provoke media opprobrium and infamy.

A strategy of violence, then, is encouraged in the Reality TV community, for the decisions on which contestants should stay and which should go is structured as a demotic decision. This is a system of judgement and classification. A vote determines who is unworthy of respect or esteem – for the contestant the outcome of the vote makes overt the fact that one's performance on the show is readable for others: the people watch you, observe you and decide upon your fate. Here, we would argue, the seemingly more fluid opportunities of celebrity identity fuse with the traces of a class-based system. There is both a celebration of aspiration (or the desire for escape from the limitations of ordinary life) and a judgmental scrutiny of the participants' behaviour – to appear too ambitious, too outrageous, too performative is to invite audience disdain. Yet to appear too dull, too isolated, too introverted, is to also invite the vote off. The conventional markers of class identity alone are inadequate here to predict who will survive and thrive in this media environment. Yet the Reality TV competition often takes place around two axes rooted in economic and social capital – that of material goods (prize money, media contracts) and that of less tangible phenomena such as popularity.

Crucial to the possession of the celebrity status that comes with popularity is a particular form of distinction in which the contestant, as he or she appears before the media audience, can be outrageous, bold, greedy, bitchy or ruthless but they cannot appear pretentious. Pretentiousness is primarily a classed charge which calls aspirant working- or lower-middle-class identities to order: 'who does she think she is kidding', 'we can see right through him'. As Steph Lawler suggests: 'pretentiousness is a charge levelled at people in whom what they *seem to be* is not (considered to be) what they are: in whom there is a gap between *being* and *seeming*'.[33] One of the pleasures of Reality TV for the audience, then, is trying to spot the gap, to see through the contestants' inauthenticity. Yet inauthenticity – the ability to put on a show – is at the same time part of the skill of the celebrity persona.

Here, as mentioned before, 'classed cross-dressing' carries with it pleasures for the aspirant celebrity subject and the media audience, but also dangers. Arrogance, outrageous or overtly ruthless behaviour can be construed as part of older established narratives of transformation in which the working-class boy or girl who wants it badly enough eventually has it all. Consequently, such behaviour signifies a desire to escape limits, to be someone, to grab a status and power normally denied. Attendant on this performance is an inevitable lack of nuance or sophistication *within the terms of class by which the contestants are constrained*. To successfully take on markers of 'cultured' identity would be to underline too clearly that class and power can be vestments or trappings rather than some integral part of one's essential identity. Classed cross-dressing then involves always the danger of discovery, of passing as one of a 'higher order'; and the attendant pleasure for the audience of unmasking someone's hubris.

The institutionalised cultural management that is at the core of celebrity culture was wedded to a new development of the Reality TV show: *The Club*. Here, we argue, the distinction between the real celebrity and the would-be celebrity and between the reality of the game and of the game as a packaged show have been further muddied. This was launched in early 2003, when Carlton broadcast a new show staged in a City bar: Nylon, a retro-themed, two floored bar in London's square mile. Each week for the duration of the six-week show, three celebrities took control of one of the bars at Nylon and their team of bartenders would battle it out to make their bar the coolest one. Each week the celebrity nominated a member of his or her team to get the sack; viewers were witness to the nomination and to the celebrity's appraisal of their staff. TV viewers were also asked to vote for the team member that they wanted to lose their job and the sacking took place live on TV. Open auditions were then held and those who voted *or who attended* the club could, if they chose, ask to be nominated to replace the sacked bar member.

Chrysalis-owned Galaxy radio network teamed up with Carlton to promote the show and when it started, its presenters, celebrity bar managers and team members featured on the dance music stations, and Galaxy DJs managed the decks at Nylon. The club had the capacity to pack in over 500 revellers.[34] It was promoted using the now-common media practice of 'emotional branding'.[35] In this case, the commodity was associated with the subjectivities of everyday working-class life. The three celebrities selected to run the bar were emblems of working-class culture made good. Samantha (Sam) Fox, the former *Sun* 'page three girl' of the 1980s, who, as the official website profile stresses, started work on the *Sun* at sixteen years of age and has gone on to make a wide-ranging showbusiness career for herself. Fox has accrued an iconic status as a former tabloid star and still signifies a brash hedonism and visual excitement combined with a determined desire for celebrity success.[36] She was presented throughout the programme as a tough achiever who combined glamour with tabloid's populist appeal. Her climb to success is marked by a significant gender and class realignment in which working-class women resist discourses of sobriety in the unashamed use of their sexuality to accrue celebrity status; a positioning which sits easily with the personas and self-professed ambitions of Reality TV's contestants.

The second bar manager was Dean Gaffney, who started work on the long-running British TV soap opera *Eastenders*, again at the early age of fifteen. Gaffney is presented as a working-class success story, which melds real-life with his soap persona. The website states that Gaffney is 'no stranger to hard and unglamorous work, and he vividly remembers pounding the pavements on his paper round as a boy'. This is immediately juxtaposed with tales of his current penchant for fast cars and drinking sessions at *Stringfellows* nightclub: 'the trials of celebrity lifestyle!' Gaffney's bar eventually won the £15,000 prize money. The third bar manager was Richard Blackwood, a former MTV presenter turned Channel 4 presenter then pop star. The web profile again presents Blackwood as a person who wants to be remembered as 'a real personality that came from nothing'.

All three bar managers reveal the use of celebrity to represent the emotion of the cultural product: they signify the importance of ambition, exceptional personality and a drive to achieve success from nothing. What is interesting is the elision between their celebrity personas and their real-life status. All three are presented as working-class without specific reference to these terms. Gaffney's soap persona is melded with his personal media achievement whilst Sam Fox exemplifies how being a working celebrity means interpreting economics in sexual as well as financial terms.

There are a number of points to be made about the innovation and self-referential and often hybrid status of *The Club*. The contestants too are mainly from fairly mundane jobs as clerical workers, bar men or women, supermarket workers and so on. They share the common desire to succeed in media terms. *The Club* breaks down the division between would-be and successful celebrity that had heretofore been maintained in, for example, the *Big Brother* and *Survivor* shows. Celebrities work alongside ordinary contestants in the bar and are overtly constructed as cultural workers with shared ambitions. Whilst the division in power is maintained – through the hierarchy of the bar managed by the established celebrity – there are moments when this breaks down. At one point, Fox's crew chastised her in the appraisal session for drinking too much and jeopardising their chances – a scene in which Sam walks off camera twice and later apologises to her team.

The contestants and celebrities challenge any easy notion of classed identity. Both in a sense occupy ersatz class positions – drawing too easily on narratives of gritty success that, in the case of the celebrities, obliterate the distinctions between their public and private personas. Both perform for camera whilst also baring their more 'authentic' anxieties about other team members in by-now well-rehearsed confessional to-camera moments that supposedly characterise Reality TV's glimpse of the authentic person.

Finally then, *The Club* erodes the division between the audience and the performers. Shows such as the USA-based *Survivor* have operated a no-fly zone over their island competition-space to exclude the danger/chaos of outsiders breaking into the reality of the mediated event. *Big Brother* shuts contestants away from the physical presence of ordinary others and opens them only to the televisual/computer gaze. In contrast, *The Club* was open to the public who could visit the club every night of the week including the televised nights. For a minimal fee they could join in the media event, buying drinks at the bar, talking with and assessing the contestants and celebrities and, if lucky, appearing on the TV screen itself. It was a rewriting of the local and particular experience of the local bar into the global distanced voyeurism of television land. If you were young enough, had some money, dressed smartly and lived in London you could inhabit a Reality TV space. This was a marked extension of the viewers' exercise of their discrimination in voting and offered the even more fleeting few seconds of media fame as the camera caught them at the bar or nearby amidst Nylon's consumers. This was Reality TV writ large, revealing how people routinely select and weave mediated, publicly available symbolic representations and discourses into their everyday lives and revealing how that participation can be packaged and sold. It points to an extension of the fantasy role that Reality TV can play in articulating social aspiration within media culture.

Notes

1. We are choosing to use the term 'celebrity' in its broadest sense of people who are objects of pronounced media attention over which they may have only a limited amount of control. We are also excluding elite persons who, for example, first come to the attention of the media and are newsworthy through their work in the traditional 'masculinised' public sphere of politics, big business or the City.
2. There is much debate about how 'new' the new forms of programming actually are. Chris Dunckley in 'It's not new and it's not clever', Institute of Ideas (ed.) *Reality TV: How Real is Real?* Hodder and Stoughton, London 2002, argues, for example, that these programmes have their roots in popular programming dating from the 1960s. Dunckley suggests that the novel aspect of these shows is that they humiliate the ordinary people who feature in them. In contrast Graham Barnfield's 'From Direct Cinema to car wreck video: Reality TV and the crisis of confidence', also in the Institute of Ideas collection, has shown how this programming has been influenced by the more respectable forms of Direct Cinema and ciné-verité and that its novelty lies in its testament to a prevailing loss of faith in objective truth. Although these writers

disagree about Reality TV's origins they both, at least, point to the ways in which these forms are innovative in their emphasis on subjective representation and relative truth, the private sphere of the personal and the emotional (on the latter see also Liesbet van Zoonen, 'Desire and resistance: *Big Brother* and the recognition of everyday life', in *Media, Culture and Society*, Vol. 23, 2001, pp669-677.

3. See for example Vivian Nicholson's well-known autobiography *Spend, Spend, Spend* (with Stephen Smith), Fontana, London 1978, which chronicles her football pools win and the subsequent notoriety that made her a media celebrity. The National Lottery was established in Britain in 1994. For accounts of lottery winners and their encounters with the media see Hunter Davies, *Living on the Lottery*, Warner Books, London 1996.
4. Photospreads of the characters from the series have, appropriately enough, appeared in *Hello!*, 14 January 2003, pp14-18.
5. *Mirror* editor Piers Morgan has described Victoria Beckham, for example, as 'the new Diana' (*Tabloid Tales*, BBC1 2003).
6. See John Langer, *Tabloid Television: Popular Journalism and the 'Other' News*, Routledge, London 1998.
7. F. Alberoni, 'The powerless elite: theory and sociological research on the phenomena of the stars', in Denis McQuail (ed.) *Sociology of Mass Communications: Selected Readings*, Penguin, Harmondsworth 1972.
8. Graeme Turner, Frances Bonner and P.D. Marshall, *Fame Games: the Production of Celebrity in Australia*, Cambridge University Press, Cambridge 2000.
9. Yvonne Tasker, *Working Girls: Gender and Sexuality in Popular Cinema*, Routledge, London 1998, p40.
10. There are a number of conflicting definitions of reality television. In the context of this article we are excluding programmes recorded 'on the wing' via CCTV or lightweight video equipment or where dramatic reconstructions play a central part e.g. *Crimewatch, CCTV TV* or *999* (see Richard Kilborn, 'How real can you get? Recent developments in "reality" television', in *European Journal of Communication*, 1994, Vol. 9, pp421-439). Our focus is on programmes such as docusoaps and reality game shows where filming is more sustained and packaged in hybrid formats that marry reality-style filming with, for example, soaps, games shows, lifestyle shows and so on.
11. Germaine Greer, 'We are Big Brother', *The Australian Media*, 12 July 2001, republished in Harold Mark (ed.), *Scum at the Top, Australia's Journal of Political Character Assassination*, Vol. 5, No.13, Melbourne: Australia, 2001 http://members.optushome.com.au/thesquiz/greer.htm accessed 3 October 2002.
12. Bob Franklin, *Newszak and News Media*, Arnold, London 1997.
13. Barnfield, op cit, p51.
14. David S. Broder in Kevin Glynn, *Tabloid Culture: Trash Taste, Popular Power, and the Transformation of American Television*, Duke University Press, Durham and London 2000, p22.
15. Julia Day, 'Channel 4: thinks big for celebrity reality show', *Guardian*, 4 November 2002, http://media.guardian.co.uk/Print/0,3858,4539336,00.html accessed 19 May 2002.
16. Langer, op cit, pp45-73.
17. Ibid, pp50-51.
18. Ibid, p46.
19. Not only achievement but also dramatic failure will bring individuals into the celebrity matrix. Most recently the attempt by Charles and Diana Ingram and their accomplice Tecwen Whittock to defraud the British quiz show *Who wants to be a Millionaire?* transformed them from celebrity winners to celebrity criminals. The documentary

Millionaire: A Major Fraud (ITV1), which broadcast the show and revealed the fraudsters' methods, shown on 21 April 2003, attracted nearly 17 million viewers, the biggest audience ever for a factual television programme on ITV.
20. Langer, op cit, p72.
21. *Pop Idol* won the prestigious Golden Rose of Montreux in 2002. It was cited by the judges as 'perfect television' (http://www.elstree.co.uk). Will Young and runner-up Gareth Gates were both given recording contracts with BMG.
22. The appeal of the competition and its lure as a springboard to celebrity status are illustrated by the number of applications to audition for the 2003 *Pop Idol*. The programme-makers Thames TV/19 TV production received over 20,000 applications just prior to the 28 February 2003 closing date. See *Pop Idol* official website 2003 http://www.itv.com/popidol/ accessed 18 March 2003.
23. Elstree Studio website http://www.elstree.co.uk/ accessed 3 October 2002.
24. Langer, op cit, p63.
25. Ibid, p72.
26. Peter Balzalgette, The Huw Weldon Lecture 2001, '*Big Brother* and Beyond', http://www.rts.org.uk/rts/html/magazine/weldon.htm accessed 3 October 2002, p.8.
27. Ibid, p2. Indeed, the figures for *Big Brother* productions are impressive. The November 2002 final of *Celebrity Big Brother* attracted nearly 50 percent of the overall primetime TV audience.
28. Fans of the third *Big Brother* spent an average of three and a half-hours a week watching the action on computers at work and home. For the 2002 *Celebrity Big Brother*, BT Broadband teamed up with Channel 4 to offer 24-hour coverage of the six celebrity housemates over their ten-day incarceration, and special desktop software was developed to update office workers with the latest significant scenes within the house. Extra footage of *Celebrity Big Brother* was streamed live on E4, the digital interactive service, and the Internet.
29. 'A case for expulsion: *Big Brother's* challenge for Channel 4', *Guardian* 31 July 2002 http://MediaGuardian.co.uk/bigbrother/story/0,7531,766576,00.html accessed 03/10/2002.
30. Annette Kuhn, *Family Secrets: Acts of Memory and Imagination*, Verso, London 1995, p98.
31. Angela McRobbie, 'Dance Narratives and Fantasies Achievement', in *Feminism and Youth Culture: From Jackie to Just Seventeen*, Macmillan Education, Basingstoke 1991, p215.
32. *Guardian*, 31st July 2002, op cit.
33. Steph Lawler, 'Escape and Escapism: Representing Working-Class Women', in Sally Munt (ed.), *Cultural Studies and the Working Class: Subject to Change*, Cassell, London 2000, p121.
34. Julia Day, 'New reality show joins The Club', *Guardian*, 22 January 2003 http://media.guardian.co.uk/broadcast/story/0,7493,879478,00.html accessed 14/05/2003, pp1-2.
35. James Lull, *Media, Communication, Culture: A Global Approach*, Polity Press, Cambridge 2000, p170.
36. Patricia Holland, 'The politics of the smile: "Soft news" and the sexualisation of the popular press', in Cynthia Carter, Gill Branston and Stuart Allan (eds.) *News, Gender and Power*, Routledge, London 1998, p24-5.

Recognition in the eyes of the relevant beholder

Representing 'subcultural celebrity' and cult TV fan cultures

Matt Hills

Academic work has often assumed that 'celebrities' are, by definition, culturally ubiquitous or generally recognised by audiences. However, this article examines celebrities who are specifically known within fan subcultures, e.g. actors linked to cult TV programmes. It considers fictional representations of cult TV celebrities and their fans, thus exploring the 'sense-making practices' surrounding 'subcultural celebrities'.

An established body of work has sought to consider the issue of celebrity/stardom, questioning myths of charisma, and viewing stars/celebrities as textual, historicised, commercial constructions of 'authenticity' and cultural power.[1] Although the phenomenon of celebrity has been variously analysed, certain assumptions have typically remained in place in this *oeuvre*.

By focusing on fans of cult TV, and their relationship to cult TV celebrities, I want to draw attention to (and challenge) one assumption which has structured work on stardom/celebrity: the assumed ubiquity of celebrities. Even where stardom/celebrity and fandom have been analysed via specific sociological factors (stars and their female fans, or stars and fans in a national context[2]), specific stars/celebrities have usually been treated as culturally ubiquitous. Stars/celebrities are hence assumed to constitute a mass-mediated and shared currency within contemporary consumer cultures. As S. Paige Baty has written:

> Representative characters such as Marilyn... allow for some familiarity in the virtual American community. *By virtue of her familiarity, Marilyn serves as a sort of cultural currency – the coin of the real.* Her name may be invoked by guests on talk shows, newspaper reporters, political commentators, and other

actors as an instantly recognisable expression of a mood, an era, a sexuality; in short, *she allows an audience to draw from a common ground of memory.*[3]

A further example of this equation between 'celebrity' and generalised audience knowledge occurs in Chris Rojek's work.[4] Rojek introduces a distinction between 'renown' and 'celebrity', suggesting that the former is 'the informal attribution of distinction on an individual within a given social network', where this 'depends on reciprocal personal or direct para-social contact'.[5] For Rojek, 'celebrity' requires distance rather than contact, and mediation rather than reciprocal presence:

> In contrast, the fame of the celebrity is ubiquitous ... Whereas renown follows from personal contact with the individual who is differentiated as unusual or unique, celebrity and notoriety assume a relationship in which the individual who is differentiated by honorific status is distanced from the spectator by stage, screen, or some equivalent medium of communication. Social distance is the precondition... of celebrity.[6]

What Rojek's distinction excludes is the possibility that between 'renown' and 'celebrity' there may exist other forms of celebrity, such as that which is characteristic of cult TV celebrities within their fan cultures. In this instance, mediation generates initial celebrity status, but this situation is then modified for cult TV fans via their personal interaction with the given celebrity. I could become a fan of a cult TV celebrity on the basis that I 'know' them through their mass-mediated existence as a text, but I may then subsequently have personal contact with this celebrity, perhaps repeatedly, at the conventions, signings, and personal appearances that form part of cult TV fan cultural activity. In this case, is the 'celebrity' only known via mass-mediation? Is this an attribution of 'celebrity' or 'renown'? Rojek's categories do not appear to remain easily separable, especially where cult TV fandoms are concerned, since the relations between these fans and celebrities may be a matter of subcultural, social knowledge and repeated personal contact *as well as* or *rather than* emerging through common cultural currency and mediated distance. This scenario can be further complicated by the fact that such 'celebrities' may no longer be appearing in any mass-mediated role. Their celebrity status, although initially dependent on mass-mediation, may in later stages of their careers be sustained primarily via direct contact with fans within a specific subculture. Any static distinction between 'renown' and 'celebrity' fails to capture temporal shifts in celebrity status, whereby some cult TV celebrities may be considered to enter 'post-fame' subcultural career phases, whilst also neglecting the fact that other celebrities who are recognised within a cult TV fan culture may never achieve wider recognition, despite appearing or working in the media industry.

What I want to argue here, then, is that it is important to theorise 'subcultural celebrities', i.e. mediated figures who are treated as famous only by and for their fan audiences. Although some previous work on celebrity has considered how audience subcultures interpret and recognise their idols in distinctive ways, such work has still tended to focus on culturally ubiquitous celebrities who are read differently by audience subcultures.[7] Academic work has not, to date, focused significantly on the *restricted celebrity status* that might be created by audience subcultures. Cult TV and its fan cultures offer one cultural site where this type of celebrity is generated and sustained, and hence will be my focal points here. Academic work has also, to date, marked out a star/celebrity distinction,[8] seeking to distinguish between a 'star' (where a star persona overshadows a diegetic role) and a 'celebrity' (where character overshadows performer). Cult TV fans are interested in celebrity and character texts, and utilise both as the basis for their fan activities, even if character-based interpretation tends to predominate.[9] Celebrity and character are treated as a complex semiotic interaction, as fans playfully negotiate lines between the two. Given that cult TV fans are interested both in the actor behind the character, and the character that an actor embodies, I will use the terms 'star' and 'celebrity' interchangeably here. I am not persuaded that the star/celebrity distinction is of much value when discussing contemporary media culture (and cult TV fan cultures specifically), given that many actors blur star personae with character constructions in a range of publicity texts.

Exceptions to the first theoretical assumption identified above – that celebrity is culturally ubiquitous – are contained in the work of Jackie Stacey and Annette Kuhn.[10] However, these exceptions are not explicitly linked to the issue of celebrity within subcultures, thus reinforcing a sense that subcultural readings are important only when they modify or oppose generalised readings of otherwise ubiquitous celebrities.

By introducing the term 'subcultural celebrity' to refer to celebrities who are not widely known, or who have moved out of a career stage of wide recognition, I am drawing on Sarah Thornton's critique of the work of sociologist Pierre Bourdieu.[11] Bourdieu conceptualised culture by using capital as a metaphor for forms of education and social contacts, termed 'cultural capital' and 'social capital' respectively. Thornton's revision of Bourdieu's work pointed out that we cannot assume that all forms of cultural knowledge, and their legitimacy, are shared by a singular, common culture.[12] Thornton coined the term 'subcultural capital', which she suggests 'confers status on its owner in the eyes of the relevant beholder'.[13] Subcultural capital is, thus, a type of knowledge which is only recognised as valuable within a subculture; this could be the knowledge displayed by cult TV fans, the knowledge of hobbyist groups such as stamp-collectors, or the expertise of music-based subcultures.

Perhaps we need to make a similar move when thinking about celebrity, considering certain celebrities not as sustaining a 'cultural currency' or 'common ground of memory', but rather as unifying subcultures of fans. In my extension of Thornton's work, then, such celebrities would be treated and recognised as celebrities only by 'the relevant beholder' (the cult TV fan here).

I will now go on to analyse some of the issues raised by 'subcultural celebrity' in relation to recent media representations of this celebrity type. My examples of subcultural celebrity and cult TV will be fictionalised ones, though it would be equally possible to explore non-fictional representations of subcultural celebrity via texts such as William Shatner's *Get A Life!*.[14]

It seems that media fictions have stolen the lead on media theory in this instance, and that while media and cultural theory has failed to address subcultural celebrity, this has nevertheless formed a topic for fictions. This suggests that many theoretical notions of celebrity are out of alignment with, if not lagging behind, pop cultural and self-reflexive explorations of cult celebrity status. As Alan McKee has observed: 'The logic of the Cultural Studies project demands that we recognise that theorizing is something that happens as much in popular culture as in academic writing; and that we cannot dismiss the thinking of those people who do not happen to be artists or academics simply for that fact'.[15]

In the next section, I will address the 'popular theorising' on subcultural celebrity that occurs in the Hollywood movie *Galaxy Quest* (1999, director: Dean Parisot), before moving on to discuss the made-for-BBC-TV film *Cruise of the Gods* (2002, director: Declan Lowney). Both films invent their own fictional, diegetic cult TV series – *Galaxy Quest* and *The Children of Castor* – complete with fan cultures and their own subcultural celebrities. Both can be textually analysed in order to illuminate the 'sense-making practices' surrounding subcultural celebrity, given that such 'texts are the material traces… left of the practices of sense-making'.[16]

Although this type of study cannot tell us how empirical cult TV fan cultures constitute and recognise actual subcultural celebrities, it can tell us how subcultural celebrity and cult TV fandom are made meaningful in media texts that are themselves partly aimed at niche, cult TV fan audiences. These are texts expected to be consumed by fans of the type that they represent: *Cruise of the Gods*, for example, was publicised on the BBC's *Cult Television* website,[17] whilst *Galaxy Quest* received coverage in niche magazines target-marketed at cult TV fans such as *Starburst*[18] as well as on the BBC's *Cult* website.[19]

Fictionalising subcultural celebrity and cult TV fans (I): Galaxy Quest

If what is distinctive about subcultural celebrity is its limited cultural circulation, usually within a fan culture,[20] then we might expect media representations of subcultural celebrity to be interwoven with representations of fandom. Indeed, popular theorising on cult TV subcultural celebrity appears to centrally invoke cultural stereotypes of cult TV fandom.

The interconnectedness of cult TV fans and their subcultural celebrities is worked through in a number of ways. Firstly, *Galaxy Quest* emphasises the lack of social distance between subcultural celebrities and their fans; it centres on a fan convention for a fictional cult TV show, dramatising the direct social interactions of celebrities and fans. Secondly, the film ultimately constructs and represents a meta-community of fans and celebrities. The cult TV fan community is thus extended so that actors and fans, producers and consumers, are resolved by the narrative into a single participatory community, one that is not divided by differences in (sub)cultural power or riven by internal hierarchies.

In this fictional representation, subcultural celebrities are depicted connotatively as versions of cult TV fans. *Galaxy Quest* concerns itself with conflicts between its diegetic group of actors who starred, some twenty years earlier, in the TV series *Galaxy Quest* (modelled on *Star Trek*). Tim Allen plays Jason Nesmith, who in turn appeared as Captain Peter Quincey Taggart in the fictional cult TV show (for which, read Captain James T. Kirk in *Star Trek*). Alan Rickman plays actor Alexander Dane, who appeared as the *Galaxy Quest* version of *Star Trek*'s Mr Spock character, Dr Lazaraus. The type of subcultural celebrity represented in *Galaxy Quest* is almost unremittingly one of post-fame subcultural celebrity; here are a group of actors who, diegetically, have no careers beyond their convention and personal appearances targeted at fans of *Galaxy Quest*. This is emphasised through the character of Dane and his resentment at having to repeat his *Galaxy Quest* catchphrase, and also through an early scene where Jason Nesmith (Allen) overhears fans criticising the *Galaxy Quest* actors: 'these guys haven't had a real acting job for twenty years, this is all they've got'.

Functioning as a kind of dramatic chorus, such dialogue reinforces *Galaxy Quest*'s initial perspective on subcultural celebrity; its actors feel no great affinity with, or respect for, their fans, and are simply taking the only work they can find. As Alan Rickman states in the publicity material 'documentary' included on the Region 2 DVD (*Galaxy Quest – On Location in Space*): 'Now the poor actors, tragic group that they are, have no life except going to conventions and opening computer stores'. Implied in Rickman's interpretation of the film, and working to cue a preferred reading, is the notion that subcultural celebrities of the *Galaxy Quest* type need to 'get a life'. Their careers are stalled and they are trading on former glories, unknown now by a wider audience but still adored by cult TV fans who haven't moved on after twenty years.

Subcultural celebrity and cult TV fandom are thus semiotically and connotatively intertwined in the film's initial representations, as the negative stereotype of the fan who needs to 'get a life'[21] is projected on to fictional subcultural celebrities. Thus, just as fans are often powerfully pathologised as regressive by a hostile broader culture,[22] so too are the actors of *Galaxy Quest* connoted as being trapped in the past.

Galaxy Quest makes use of the contradictory range of connotations that circulate around cult TV fandom. The film suggests, rather more positively, that subcultural celebrities should come to resemble their fans in ways that exceed the pathologising 'get a life!' stereotype: i.e. by developing textual knowledge that is akin to fan knowledge, and by relying on fan communities.

From an initial scenario where the diegetic actors are unlike their fictional counterparts, and are partly semiotically contrasted to their fans through actor/fan oppositions such as 'disinterest/enthusiasm' and 'textual ignorance/knowledge', a multiple narrative resolution is effected whereby distances between actors, their roles, and their fans are all effaced. The reconciliation of fan and actorly identities is effected primarily through the characters of Guy (Sam Rockwell) and Brandon (Justin Long), and the ways in which subcultural celebrities such as Nesmith react to these fictional fans. The character of Guy most obviously mediates the roles of 'fan' and 'actor', since he is a fan (first shown introducing the other actors at the fan convention) who also played a bit part in the series *Galaxy Quest*.

Neither aligned clearly with 'fan' or 'actor' identities, Guy is represented as constantly failing to fit in with the film's other subcultural celebrities; unlike them, he is *not* subculturally recognised (by the concluding convention compere who dubs him 'another shipmate', or by the Thermians, the alien race who treat *Galaxy Quest* as if it were a set of 'historical documents'). Also unlike the other subcultural celebrities, Guy constantly draws on his fan knowledge to self-referentially comment on narrative conventions of the original show. When the *Galaxy Quest* actors encounter a race of seemingly cute aliens, Guy remonstrates fannishly with them by pointing out that these aliens will, in all probability, turn out to be vicious and violent: 'Did you guys ever *watch* the show?'

As the other actors become more attuned to Guy's hybridised fan-actor role (i.e. as they become more fan-like) then they demonstrate 'real' heroics by beginning to draw on fan knowledge of *Galaxy Quest*; Nesmith and Dane, for example, re-perform a scene from 'episode seventeen' in order to escape from villainous henchmen, while Dane eventually re-performs Dr Lazarus's catchphrase with a fan's sincerity rather than with actorly resentment. Ultimately, Guy is shown to achieve his aim of becoming a subcultural celebrity; he is included in the cast of a new version of *Galaxy Quest*, shifting from fan-actor to fully-fledged actor and performing the fan's fantasy of entering the diegesis of a text he has loved.

The film's use of the character of Brandon is also an interesting attempt at revaluing fandom and subcultural celebrity at one and the same time. Subcultural celebrity becomes connotatively less 'sad' as cult TV fandom is semiotically revalued across the narrative, meaning that the majority of negative fan stereotypes occur in the film's opening sequences.[23]

Brandon is represented as being part of a fan community that values *Galaxy Quest* for its representations of technology – something that corresponds to an actual fan interpretive community surrounding *Star Trek*.[24] The first meeting between Brandon and Nesmith is characterised by Nesmith's refusal to perceive any value in this fan's interpretation of *Galaxy Quest*. In an intertextual reference to William Shatner's *Saturday Night Live* sketch in which he told *Star Trek* fans 'Get a life, will you people? I mean, I mean, for crying out loud, it's just a TV show!',[25] Nesmith aims almost the exact same dialogue at Brandon's technical questions about *Galaxy Quest*. Initially dismissing the fan as someone who takes the TV show too seriously, Nesmith eventually relies on Brandon to help save the NSEA Protector (the fictional show's version of *Star Trek*'s USS Enterprise). Brandon's knowledge of fictional technologies is narratively validated by *Galaxy Quest*, as he and his online fan community assist Nesmith. Fans at first represented via negative stereotypes as 'obsessive' and 'incapable of telling fantasy and reality apart' are thus revalued as heroes, but only at a narrative moment when the film's subcultural celebrities are beginning to become both positively more fan-like and also more like their heroic *Galaxy Quest* characters.

The semiotic contradictions in the film are best captured in a scene where Nesmith enlists Brandon's help. The young fan reminds the actor that he's 'not a complete braincase', but reacts to Nesmith's interruption – 'It's all real' – with a display of jubilance. The represented fan's joy at being able to enter the world of his beloved cult TV series is a moment that affectively disrupts the discourses being drawn on at this point in the narrative; Brandon is simultaneously both a fan-hero, 'not a braincase', *and* the stereotyped fan who 'knew' a cult TV show was actually real. Brandon is both negative stereotype and revalued fan, unlike the film's subcultural celebrities who are more unproblematically reconstituted as heroes. Although subcultural celebrities can apparently become more *connotatively* fan-like as they become more heroic, it seems that *denotative* representations of cult TV fandom possess less semiotic malleability: the meanings attached to characters explicitly identified as fans in the film are restricted, and always remain at least partly negative. *Galaxy Quest* moves from its initial representation of fans as morons to, at best, a situation where fans become oxymorons; simultaneously both heroes and negative stereotypes.

It is also rather problematic that only one fan interpretive community is significantly revalued by *Galaxy Quest*; female fan interpretive communities who read *Galaxy Quest* through codes of romance, watching for whether or not Captain Peter Quincey Taggart and Tawny Madison (played by Gwen Demarco, in turn played by Sigourney Weaver) have a 'thing', are validated by the film's closing clinch between actors, but their fandom is not heroically repositioned in the way that Brandon's masculinised fan reading strategy is. Just as there are limits to academic theorising on celebrity (especially the lack of work on subcultural rather than ubiquitous celebrity) so too there are limits to popular theorising on subcultural celebrity.

One further limit is marked out by the fact that it is only the character of Guy (Rockwell) whose fandom appears to become univocally positive, or valued, in *Galaxy Quest*. But we should recall that his character functions from the outset as a fan-actor; connotations of 'professional' identity and a career logic spare this representation of fandom from appearing to be either moronic or oxymoronic. Fandom is thus most significantly revalued in the film when it can be completely detached from the world of consumerism or leisure and fixed as part of a career progression. The fictionalised fan 'gets a life' by getting an actor's job, and represented subcultural celebrities get their lives back by virtue, ultimately, of getting back into the media. Although differences in cultural power are defused by these textual attempts to blend fan and actor identities, media power – the naturalised distinction between producers and consumers, or between 'media people' and 'ordinary' people – remains unchallenged here.[26] If one attraction of films like *Galaxy Quest* lies in their semiotic closing of the gap between celebrities and fan audiences via the figure of the subcultural celebrity, it seems (rather paradoxically) to be the case that such films work, finally, to naturalise representational distinctions between 'media' people and cult TV fans who are excluded from a glamorous, extraordinary media world. Even while fans and subcultural celebrities are drawn connotatively closer, each figure working to partly legitimate the other, they are left denotatively worlds apart. Only fictionalised fans already having professional access to media worlds (and already hybridised as fan-actors) are able, like Guy, to definitively cross the line between cultural producer and fan consumer in *Galaxy Quest*.

In the following discussion, I will consider how the UK production *Cruise of the Gods* treads similar ground to *Galaxy Quest*. However, it also represents very different 'popular theorising' on the matter of subcultural celebrity.

Fictionalising subcultural celebrity and cult TV fandom (II): 'The Children of Castor'

Like *Galaxy Quest*, *Cruise of the Gods* (hereafter *Cruise* …) is also a comedy-drama; it seems that neither cult TV fandom nor subcultural celebrity can be taken entirely seriously within popular cultural representations. Cult TV fandom's negative stereotypes remain so heavily prevalent within the broader culture, that it is almost as if such fandom can only be revalued under the condition that it is simultaneously mocked, remaining oxymoronic as it is caught between actual fan subcultural desires for positive representation and cultural stereotypes stressing fan 'weird geekiness'.

In *Galaxy Quest* subcultural celebrity is represented monolithically: all the *Galaxy Quest* actors were once widely known, but are now holding on to the past and clinging to their fan cultural celebrity, while bit-part player Guy is unknown even within the fan culture. However, *Cruise ...* complicates this representation, and this way of thinking about subcultural celebrities linked to its fictional UK cult TV series *The Children of Castor*. It distinguishes not so much between actors, fans and fan-actors, but rather between fans and different types of subcultural celebrities. Distinctions are semiotically mapped onto specific characters; Nick Lee (played by Steve Coogan) has gone on to find post-'Children of Castor' fame in Hollywood. Meanwhile, Andy Van Allen (Rob Brydon), who played the lead role of Romak in *Children of Castor*, now works as a hotel porter and lacks any contemporary, generalised celebrity. Like the actors of *Galaxy Quest*, Van Allen is represented as a comic-tragic figure whose career has never moved on; he is the subcultural celebrity *par excellence*. Van Allen is recognised by the *Children of Castor* Fan Club, but is seemingly unknown outside of this fan culture, having no current mass-mediated celebrity status. This mismatch between fan adulation and generalised lack of recognition is dramatised repeatedly in the film. When Van Allen is known to be on the fan cruise, fans erupt into ecstatic applause; a medium shot displaying these fans' standing ovation is intercut with close-ups of specific fans seeming to be in rapture. In marked contrast to this fan reception – 'Oh God! He's on the boat! Bloody God, he's on this boat!! ... Andy Van Allen is on the boat', announces Jeff Monks, President of the *Castor* Fan Club – Andy is treated as a nobody when he takes part in Nick Lee's hit US show 'Sherlock Holmes in Miami', and is mocked when he attends a cruise meal at the captain's table. Nick Lee (the generalised celebrity) is, however, shown to be treated with reverence by fans and non-fans alike.

Cruise ... does not just textually contrast representations of ubiquitous and subcultural celebrity. It also treats diegetic 'bit-part performers' as further examples of subcultural celebrity, unlike *Galaxy Quest*'s representation of Guy who is denied such status. In this respect, *Cruise ...* offers a different representation of cult TV fan cultures, in which fans are likely to have knowledge of, and follow, the later careers of almost every member of their show's production team, including actors/performers who appeared in very minor roles. This view of cult TV fan cultures, in which it is not just lead actors who are lionised and treated as celebrities, but also writers, is represented via two further characters in *Cruise ...*: Hugh Bispham (played by Philip Jackson) and Graham Ball (Niall Buggy). Bispham was the writer of *Children of Castor*, and like Andy Van Allen, has gone on to have no discernible later career, while Graham played no significant ongoing role in *Children of Castor* beyond appearing in the (fictional) programme's title sequence portentously intoning 'I'm changing! I'm changing!'. Although Van Allen mocks this fact when assessing his fellow cruise celebrities, muttering 'you got the bloke off the title sequence', it is repeatedly apparent that the film's fictional fans accord Graham as much respect as they do Van Allen. Graham is known to these fans; their affection for 'their' cult TV series extends to all aspects of that show, and to all personnel involved with it. Graham is thus represented as being a subcultural celebrity in a very different way to Van Allen and Bispham; unlike the lead actor, he would never have been known or recognised by non-fans, and unlike the writer, he would never have been known within the media industry. The character of Graham should seemingly be at the bottom of the subcultural celebrity heap, lacking any kind of professional identity or textual centrality in relation to *Children of Castor*. And yet, it is implied through this character that subcultural celebrity is thoroughly egalitarian rather than hierarchical. Although Van Allen is obsessed with his lack of celebrity status in comparison with the generalised celebrity 'success' of Nick Lee, the fictionalised fans make no hierarchical distinction between their subcultural celebrities, meaning that they do not refer to Andy's lack of career, and neither do they construct a hierarchy between Ball, Bispham, Lee, and Van Allen. Rather than magically resolving cultural differences between fans and celebrities, as *Galaxy Quest* does, this text works representationally to indicate that subcultural celebrity, while being restricted to a fan culture, operates entirely generally within that culture, emerging through a non-hierarchical bestowal of honour. Recognition thus appears to be conferred via a general contagion of affect rather than through a calculative logic over who has contributed the most to the cult TV series *Children of Castor*. Anyone linked to the show is depicted as deserving of fan devotion. By contrast, even subcultural celebrity is rigidly hierarchical in the Hollywood fantasy of *Galaxy Quest*; Guy is a nobody, while the crew of the NSEA Protector are the fans' heroes.

In *Cruise ...*, the represented subcultural celebrities of Graham and Hugh Bispham become focal points for specific explorations of fan-celebrity relations. Again unlike *Galaxy Quest*, this representational economy does not seek to efface cultural differences and distinctions between subcultural celebrities and fans. Aspects of *Galaxy Quest*'s symbolic logic are retained – the drama concludes with fans and celebrities united in re-enactment of an episode, both participating as equals, and tensions between Lee and Van Allen are eventually smoothed over as they too come to represent a version of fan community. Focusing only on these dimensions, we might conclude that *Cruise ...* performs the same semiotic manoeuvres as *Galaxy Quest*, finally transferring positive discourses of fandom (as enthusiastic participatory community) connotatively on to subcultural celebrities, and magically uniting fans and actors within a fictional meta-community. Although elements of this project appear in both films, *Cruise ...* does not build as seamlessly to such a narrative conclusion as its Hollywood counterpart. Instead, via the figures of Bispham and Graham, the issue of fan cultural power is raised. If fans confer celebrity status on actors who are not generally recognised as (ubiquitous) celebrities then what might this mean for (sub)cultural power relations between fans and actors?

Julie Burchill has argued that fans may favour 'hackstars' over 'genius' stars/celebrities:

> Being a fan of an entertainer of genius can be an unrewarding business – you can withdraw your support at a moment's notice and lack of it won't make your target any less of a genius. But if you are a fan of a hackstar, you have power – you and others like you can choose to stop listening/laughing/buying and the glorified nonentity will have nothing left, for when he ceases to please he ceases to exist. People appreciate this feeling of vicarious power, and feel well disposed towards those who give it to them.[27]

Cruise ... suggests that this sense of fan 'vicarious power' is attested to in the case of subcultural celebrities. The film's fictional fans have the subcultural power to elevate Graham Ball to celebrity status on the basis of his one line of dialogue, and they also have the subcultural power to elevate Hugh Bispham's work to the level of 'genius' rather than hack writing.

This represented fan subcultural power is akin to what John Tulloch describes as actual cult TV fans' 'power to gloss',[28] by which he means that fans have the (sub)cultural power to interpret 'their' show in certain ways. However, Tulloch does not explicitly address how this restricted power may also be linked to the constitution of subcultural celebrity, such that fans may not just have the discursive power to read cult TV in certain ways,[29] they may also potentially possess the subcultural, social power to confer celebrity status on 'honoured' media production personnel and actors. This potential type of social, subcultural power is represented via a moment of crisis in *Cruise* ..., as the interpretation of Fan Club President, Jeff, is challenged by Bispham, the show's writer. Where the fictionalised 'executive fan'[30] reads *Children of Castor* character names as complex meditations on mythological sources, a drunken Bispham announces that all the leads' names were anagrams of curries; Romak = Korma, Damsar = Madras, and so on. *Galaxy Quest* studiously avoids representing any such direct challenge to fan cultural activities on the part of media professionals. By doing so, *Cruise* ... complicates its imagined union of fans and subcultural celebrities, self-reflexively implying that this union can only ever be, precisely, imagined.

Fan interpretations are, ultimately, valued over professional self-accounts in the text; Bispham is censured for his disruption of fan subcultural power. The threat raised here is that his subcultural celebrity status may be revoked by executive fans, that is, fans who run the fan club. Bispham is compelled to choose between agreeing with the fan interpretation of his work (in which case *Children of Castor* remains a subtle, complex work of art, and Bispham retains his 'honoured' status), or asserting his own 'truth', in which case, as Russell the Fan Club's treasurer puts it: 'I'd have to conclude you were a talentless shit, but I prefer to think of you as a genius – what do you think?'. In this instance, Burchill's contrast between 'hackstars' and 'genius' entertainers doesn't quite capture what is at stake in this representation of subcultural celebrity; the point appears, rather, to be that it is fans who have the power to make and break 'their' celebrities by subculturally attributing powers of 'genius' to them. Burchill assumes that celebrities either display objective genius, or are 'nonentities', rather than addressing 'genius' as a communal ascription that can be policed by subcultural, executive fans who possess greater social power within their fan culture.

The representation of Graham also theorises cult TV fans' subcultural power to ascribe celebrity status, although in a different way to the fan-professional interpretive clash between Jeff Monks and Hugh Bispham. In this instance, fans are shown as conferring celebrity status on Graham, who experiences this as a kind of blessing. To describe the euphoric feeling of becoming a celebrity, Graham 'textually poaches' his own single line of dialogue – 'I'm changing! I'm changing!' – by appropriating this within his everyday life.[31] Graham uses these words to express the fact that he has been transformed by his subcultural celebrity status; changing from someone who will not be missed after his death into someone who will be mourned and treasured by *Castor* fans.

Fans on the cruise are depicted as constantly appropriating catchphrases and dialogue from *The Children of Castor*: Monks teases Andy Van Allen about eating potato, given that one infamous line from the (fictional) show runs 'When will we learn the lessons of… potato?'; the fan Jenny asks Van Allen to 'say something as Romak' while they are having sex, and Romak's catchphrase is reiterated at various points – 'What is the point of being human if we can't be humane?'. All this textual play is meant to capture actual cult fans' activity of appropriation, as they 'transform a work into a cult text' by 'break[ing], dislocat[…ing], unhing[…ing] it so that' they 'can remember… parts of it, irrespective of their original relationship with the whole'.[32] Among this constant citation and textual poaching, it is striking that Graham is shown behaving like the perfect fan at the moment that he seeks to articulate what he has been unable to say in person (and what he has recorded as a message to be played after his death). This character expresses himself poignantly and forcefully by recontextualising his *Castor* lines, shifting their meaning and affective coloration from generic, melodramatic observation to a moving acceptance of his own impending death. In this instance, *Castor* fandom's ascription of subcultural celebrity acts as a type of personal salvation; Graham's life is given significance by the fan community's production of his 'honoured' status, and as he becomes most fan-like. In a bittersweet irony, Graham 'gets a life' as the object of fan value and respect just as he is dying of cancer. He passes away as 'a King' among his fans rather than being remembered only as 'the manager of a carpet warehouse'. Attacking the stereotype of fans as wasting their time in obsessive and pointless activity, this represents cult TV fandom as a redeeming force that is subculturally powerful in terms of its ability to confer status on actors and performers, even those who might be marginal to a text's production.

Where *Galaxy Quest* culminates in an affectively-loaded moment of recognition passing between hierarchically-validated performer (Nesmith) and fan (Brandon), *Cruise* ... similarly indicates that performers and fans can achieve moments of mutual recognition, but in a rather different way. Here, this recognition is non-hierarchical, and it is the fans who, in a subculturally powerful act of recognition, confer status on the 'genius' Hugh Bispham and the respected Graham Ball. By contrast, the Hollywood text naturalises subcultural celebrity as a privileged, 'meritocratic' position that deigns to recognise fan contributions. The *Galaxy Quest* actors have to prove themselves as *Galaxy Quest*'s heroes before they can recognise their fans, and before they can deserve their fans' applause. *Cruise* ..., meanwhile, puts forward a popular theory of fan subcultural power where fans possess the very power to confer 'subcultural celebrity'. Such celebrities, in this instance, do not have to prove themselves hierarchically or naturally worthy of fan recognition; instead, this honoured status is granted automatically, and is only threatened with withdrawal if the celebrity should challenge the norms of fan activities. Despite their similarities, I have argued here that these texts – one which creates *Star Trek*-type US cult TV, and the other which creates its own *Blake's 7/Survivors*-style British cult TV – presuppose and represent almost opposed ethics of subcultural celebrity via their popular theorising.

I would suggest that this representational difference illustrates an essential problematic in the 'sense-making practices' surrounding subcultural celebrity. Unlike generalised or ubiquitous celebrity, which exceeds any one authorising fan culture, this specific phenomenon is produced as a matter of fan subcultural power. But if actual fan cultures misrecognise their attributive power, they risk fetishising their own created celebrities. This 'celebrity fetish' is represented in *Galaxy Quest*, where monolithic subcultural celebrities are mythically positioned as the authentic source of their fan adulation, since they become 'truly' heroic rather than being divided between character/actor identities. Yet such a 'celebrity fetish' is challenged in *Cruise of the Gods*, where different types of subcultural celebrity are accorded equal fan adulation, and are represented as the product of fan cultural activity rather than as a precondition for this activity. *Galaxy Quest* (1999) and *Cruise of the Gods* (2002) can be thought of as participating in an intertextual conversation, as staging a debate – within popular culture – over how we might theorise and represent the activities of cult TV fans via the existence of their non-ubiquitous, subcultural celebrities.

Notes

All websites accessed April 2003.

1. See Leo Braudy, *The Frenzy of Renown*, Oxford University Press 1986; Jeremy Butler (ed), *Star Texts: Image and Performance in Film and Television*, Wayne State University Press 1991; Richard Dyer, *Stars*, BFI Publishing 1979; Joshua Gamson, *Claims to Fame: Celebrity in Contemporary America*, University of California Press 1994; Christine Gledhill (ed), *Stardom: Industry of Desire*, Routledge 1991; P. David Marshall, *Celebrity and Power: Fame in Contemporary Culture*, University of Minnesota Press 1997; Graeme Turner, Frances Bonner and P. David Marshall, *Fame Games: The Production of Celebrity in Australia*, Cambridge University Press 2000.
2. See Rachel Moseley, *Growing Up with Audrey Hepburn*, Manchester University Press 2002; Sarah Street, *British Cinema in Documents*, Routledge 2000.
3. S. Paige Baty, *American Monroe: The Making of a Body Politic*, University of California Press 1995 pp39-40, my italics.
4. Chris Rojek, *Celebrity*, Reaktion Books 2001.
5. Ibid p12.
6. Ibid p12.
7. See Richard Dyer, *Heavenly Bodies*, BFI Publishing 1986, where the subcultural readings of gay men are considered; or Michael DeAngelis, *Gay Fandom and Crossover Stardom*, Duke University Press 2001, where publicity practices are said to facilitate the 'queering' of certain celebrities within gay subcultural readings.
8. See John Ellis, *Visible Fictions*, Routledge 1992.
9. See Sara Gwenllian Jones, 'Starring Lucy Lawless?', *Continuum*, Vol. 14, No. 1, 2000, p12.
10. See Jackie Stacey, *Star Gazing: Hollywood cinema and female spectatorship*, Routledge 1994; Annette Kuhn, *An Everyday Magic: Cinema and Cultural Memory*, I.B. Tauris 2002.
11. Sarah Thornton, *Club Cultures*, Polity Press 1995.
12. See Matt Hills, *Fan Cultures*, Routledge 2002, Chapter 2.
13. Thornton op cit p11.
14. William Shatner with Chris Kreski, *Get A Life!*, Simon and Schuster 1999.
15. Ian McKee, 'What Cultural Studies Needs Is More Theory', *Continuum*, Vol. 16, No. 3, 2002 p315.
16. Alan McKee, *Textual Analysis*, Sage 2003 p15.
17. See 'Fandom and fame sent-up in a BBC comedy special', http://www.bbc.co.uk/cult/news/02112702.shtml
18. See http://www.visimag.com/starburst/261_feature.htm
19. http://www.bbc.co.uk/cult/st/interviews/stewart/page13.shtml
20. Although academic celebrities may also be thought of as not usually achieving recognition outside academic subcultures; see Joe Moran, *Star Authors*, Pluto Press 2000 pp155-161.
21. See Henry Jenkins, *Textual Poachers*, Routledge 1992, pp9-15.
22. See Joli Jenson, 'Fandom As Pathology', in Lisa A Lewis (ed) *The Adoring Audience*, Routledge 1992.
23. And often through the coded figures of the alien Thermians, such that Nesmith, confused as to the alien race involved, says of one Thermian, 'she's not a fan... she's a termite'. Despite the fact that these aliens clearly connote fandom's negative stereotypes – they are socially awkward, child-like and can't tell fantasy from reality – they are explicitly denied the denotative status of 'fans'.

24. See John Tulloch and Henry Jenkins, *Science Fiction Audiences*, Routledge 1995, Chapter 11.
25. See Henry Jenkins, *Textual Poachers*, Routledge 1992, pp9-10.
26. See Nick Couldry, *The Place of Media Power*, Routledge 2000, on media power conceptualised in this way.
27. Julie Burchill, *Damaged Gods: Cults and Heroes Reappraised*, Century 1986, pp141-2.
28. See John Tulloch and Henry Jenkins, *Science Fiction Audiences*, Routledge 1995, pp147.
29. Ibid p150.
30. Ibid p149.
31. See Henry Jenkins, *Textual Poachers*, Routledge 1992, on fan appropriations of cult TV texts.
32. See Umberto Eco, *Faith in Fakes*, Minerva 1995, p198.

Pop stars who can't act
The limits of celebrity 'multi-tasking'

Kay Dickinson

This article situates the phenomenon of artists who cross over from musical stardom into cinema within the context of the horizontal integration of the entertainment industries. An attention to singers who are considered to act badly opens out an exploration of how each sphere of production (music and film) regulates and organizes what it considers to be valuable and extra-ordinary work, and how these might prove incompatible when allied with other artistic activities. The popular discourses circulating around such performances are illuminating in what they reveal about pervasive anxieties and debates about what currently constitutes our understanding of labour.

There is much talk these days about multi-platform entertainment products and producers, but relatively less rumination on the instances where these diverse yet interlinked commodities appear ill-conceived in the eyes of the buying public. This dissatisfaction seems to occur on a fairly regular basis when established pop stars try their luck in movies. Admittedly, there are hosts of successful artists criss-crossing between film and music: Cher, for instance. There are also examples where famous singers with perhaps limited acting capabilities are 'well used' because their standard personae helpfully overlap with the film roles in which they have been cast (such as David Bowie in *The Man Who Fell to Earth* (Roeg, 1976)). However, with this article, I want to mull over the crossover failure, the pop star who 'can't act'. These cases often provoke overblown and vitriolic reactions from critics and viewing public alike, telling us much about how we currently define the concepts and practices of labour.

Two newspaper articles responding to *Honest* (Stewart, 2000) – a vehicle for the three white members of the girl group All Saints – encapsulate a widespread contempt for the inadequate singer-turned-actor. This is Richard Benson from *The Independent*: 'It is just as awful as we thought, even as awful as we hoped it would be when we learned that the Appleton sisters were "starring" in it.'[1] Thomas Quinn from *The Mirror* concludes his review of the film with: 'Weighing it all up, maybe all these rockers aren't completely off their, ahem, rockers to try their hand at the movies. At least we all get a good laugh when they get it spectacularly wrong.'[2] Although these two papers rarely share similar outlooks on popular culture, they are united (as I am sure are much of the entertainment-consuming public) in a malicious eagerness to watch these up-start thespians blunder, whatever respect they might or might not have for them as musicians. The few begging to differ are usually the die-hard devotees of the musician *qua* musician, people who can affirm their loyalty and the strength of their fan identity by blindly loving these performances regardless – and, of course, by willingly buying the augmented range of media products that such crossovers generate.

However, I do not wish to dwell on these audiences or to prioritise a study of the proliferating means by which crossover products are invented, marketed and consumed. Instead, I am curious about the *work* that is being done here and how such performances open up and fall into a variety of discourses about contemporary labour systems. Such a task becomes distinctly more demanding when it becomes apparent that both music and film stars are strangely indeterminate figures: it is hard to ascertain whether they are labour or capital, producers or commodities.[3] To an extent, they/their personae are manufactured and sold, yet the performers themselves are also essential to the active creative process. Moreover, as Danae Clark observes of classical Hollywood movie actors (and the same could be said of popular musicians), stars embody a profitably ambiguous relationship between 'the real' and the fabricated and mass reproduced:

> the fruits of labour produced a commodity that was particularly rich in surplus value. Even though the image or star icon was dislocated from the sphere of production, its representational form appeared to capture 'the real thing' thus providing a strong source of fetishistic attachment with which to link the consumer to the actor's body in the sphere of circulation.[4]

What this abstracted essence might represent and how its semantics might be demarcated by other producers and consumers is the meat of most scholarly literature on the topic, especially the kind which follows in the tradition of Richard Dyer's *Stars*[5] (and valuable analysis it is too). Coming from a slightly different angle, however, it is just as vital to scrutinise our relationship with the work that is seen to be done by the star-as-person; to concentrate on what they *do* as well as what they are. A divergence between these two actions (so often underplayed, as I will go on to argue, by the entertainment industries), is particularly glaring in the case of the lack-lustre crossover star. In this instance, 'being' is not enough (except for the most forgiving of fans) and, in not having completed the expected actorly work, the musician reminds us that, whilst watching movies, we are paying for a service, a job of work (albeit recorded), as well as a neatly packaged commodity fetish.

In order to unravel these distinctions, though, and begin to analyse how and why such performances are rated, it is necessary to ascertain where the professions of acting and music-making peg out their boundary-lines of acceptable work. A definition of 'bad acting' – below par labour – needs firstly to consider the dominant kinds of performance associated with mainstream cinema. As Paul McDonald points out, 'The question of believability in acting is only at issue where film performers are placed in the formal conventions of realist narrative cinema.'[6] The hegemonic power of this ultimately highly coded system of representation lies in its claims to be simultaneously vitally connected to our everyday lives ('realist'), but also – in case we begin to interrogate it too closely – fantasy and entertainment ('fiction'). Actorly skills in maintaining this equilibrium have, unsurprisingly, been inscribed into the professional requirements these cinemas use to regulate and perpetuate themselves, to make themselves understood and, by implication, to suggest the incomprehensibility or incompetence of other forms of film communication. Given the complicity of most movie consumers in these markers of quality acting, the best most performers can do to break from such limitations – should they want to – is to 'prove' themselves capable of realist acting, and then move 'beyond' it. The fact that the All Saints women have neglected to leap through this first essential hoop means that the unease and lack of fabricated transparency in their performances could never be interpreted as deliberately and defiantly anti-realist – it is just 'wrong'.

Instead of smoothly slipping into this bizarre, inconsistent projection of realism, pop stars are regularly unable to immerse themselves fully in characterisation, largely because they are too obtrusively 'themselves' (ironically, too 'real') to mingle inconspicuously with the illusionist world of the film's diegesis. As David Thompson observes, 'A pop persona works in a different way from a film persona: it is *more* complete, which means it's harder to submerge and keeps popping up at the wrong moment.'[7] Even pop's most adamant chameleons (such as Madonna or Lou Reed) sustain their chosen colours too consistently and whole-heartedly to comply with the mutability required by realist acting, although such timing is perhaps essential for successful musical career building.

Yet surely accepted film stars also often break through the narrative facade without such actions adding up to bad acting? Throughout the history of Hollywood film-making, successful acting has been about apportioning equal attention to losing oneself in the role and upholding a singular star presence which can induce interest (and money) beyond the film text. Quite often the 'failure' of pop star-actors rests on their assertion of this latter quality – the instantly recognisable and more constant sense of star persona – and thus the ratio of 'absence' to 'presence' becomes unfavourably distributed. Moreover, these gaps are often eagerly welcomed by the industry, vital as they are for the creation of sundry commodities which promise to span the chasms which separate acting roles from a star's 'real life'.

However, these connections between film appearance and outside world marketability function in yet another fashion with musician-actors. The constant reminders that the star is not a 'real actor' reinforces – even whilst we may be trying to envelope ourselves in a cinematic narrative – the knowledge of what they 'really' are. Whilst this jeopardises the success of the film and the respect the star may garner, the promotional wings of the entertainment industry gain, almost regardless of the film's critical outcome. If these stars are seemingly out of context, we try to put them back in their places. As we are watching or discussing these films, we are simultaneously considering the music industry, its workers, the artist's worth, their other oeuvre and their talent. If nothing else, the dislocation of the musician-actor asks us to snap them, and ourselves, back into the world of their more reliable produce.

And this asks for a reinvestment in the music industry's own systems of stardom, ones which are distinctly divergent from those to which movie actors might adhere. Time and time again, especially within the more revered genres of popular music, personae are built upon notions of personal integrity, of binding one's innermost feelings to one's work, and refusing to be party to anything which is thought to be 'untrue' to themselves (this would include such things as miming on stage). Certainly there are pop stars who work in more collaborative or consciously 'artificial' ways, but, so strong is the image of the Authentic Artist, that musicians of this ilk are constantly being asked to defend themselves or to admit their inferiority as 'manufactured' entities. Such a logic is much more marginal to the work of acting where an aptitude for deviating from 'the self' is written into the job description.

Correspondingly, since at least the 1960s, pop stars have had an even greater duty than screen stars to bond their performance personalities to their off-stage activities. The Romantic ideal of artistic material perfectly corresponding to a unique personal creativity (preferably one which endures suffering) is a much more central bulwark to popular music stardom. While movie actors are often at pains to disentangle themselves from the limited, mythic values they stand for on screen, a musician is under a certain amount of pressure to live out their 'rock'n'roll-ness' beyond the realms of the 9-5. This reflects the infusive properties of the rock (and Romantic) tradition, whose oeuvre is less a body of artistic material and more a 'way of life' than most mainstream cinema (cult films aside) has ever dreamt of being. In fact, it is fairly common for musical stars who are trying to expose the 'performative' elements of their star incarnations to impersonate a string of famous film stars (Madonna, for instance, does this), perhaps as a way of trying to loosen the shackles of musical star inscription.

Conversely, many successful actors prefer to flag up the discrepancies between on-screen role and off-screen self, precisely because such variance emphasises the acting skills involved in transforming between the two. On the other hand, the consistency of the musician identity highlights how relatively recent (and perhaps how linked to post-industrial capitalist inscriptions of labour and leisure) the concepts of being on- and off-duty are. Whilst such jobs are residual legacies of all-encompassing vocations of the past, such as the court composer or the wandering minstrel, they are also widely enviable in a current climate where there is, as Angela McRobbie observes, '[an] encroachment of work into every corner of everyday life, including "flexible" working at home, "sociable" working in cafes with plug-in points for laptops, and mobile working from indeterminate "non-places".'[8] That leisure and labour could be indistinguishable, that one would *choose* to be working hard because the job is so fulfilling in itself, is a common fantasy when over-time is more an inevitable encroachment of an increasingly unregulated post-Fordist corporate buyers' market. To always be 'at work', but for that work to incorporate decadence and creativity, is certainly central to the fact that large numbers of people dream of pop stardom.

Considering these working conditions, it is hardly surprising that the process of 'crossing over', of departing the music world and all it purports to stand for, is often a manoeuvre fraught with difficulties, not least those provoked by a sense of loyalty to one's art form. The counter-cultural posturing of many post-60s musicians, particularly those associated with rock, makes them (and many musicians since) wary of edging into cinema. Film is often claimed to be staid; to appear in a movie may even be tantamount to 'selling out'. And 'selling' is central to this philosophy, which strangely sees music production as anti-capitalist and which mocks or pities musicians who dance between formats to the tune of a ringing cash register. The most precious case study, and cautionary tale, for advocates of such ideas is that of an artistically imprisoned Elvis Presley, desperate to break free from the meaninglessness of movie-making in order to do what really mattered: recording music. Whilst the mechanisms of both entertainment industries throw up questions of star control due to their fragmented means of production, music has a much more central history of critiquing such modes of production, even downplaying their existence. Indeed, open hostility to such modes of manufacture is pervasive in rock music, propounded not only in such things as interviews, but also in song lyrics themselves. This stance is regularly adopted regardless of the concurrent compatibility between consumer capitalism and the kinds of Romantic individualism that rock holds so dear. At the very least, whilst rock stars vigorously defend their own working rights, their buying practices rarely stretch such ethics into a consideration of the injustices of other people's labour conditions.

Evidently, then, a musician's public personality cannot sincerely hold itself up to be some sort of coherent and unmediated essentialist self. It is surely as fabricated a role as any other and just as prone to external interpellations of stardom, not least as a result of the corporate work undergone on it in order to create profit. Moreover, musical stardom requires training, perseverance and adherence to tradition. Such factors are, as I have suggested, at odds with the narrative flow of most films, rendering the singer-actor frequently bewildered and out of place. What might the more specific rules of musical-performance-as-work have to do with this disjunction? One important factor to consider is that popular music's ways of creating meaning are largely resistant to prolonged and teleological story-telling. Meaning within many musical genres is, for the most part, constructed out of A, B and C units which, unlike those of film, are repeated at least once and do not conventionally travel down a one-way narrative path.

Moreover, the acting style which pop stars are the most accustomed to is the type required for music videos. Digressing from the mainstays of narrative realism, this is a technique which must withstand rapid-fire editing and thematic lurches (those that mark the shift from verse to chorus, for instance). Meanings are much more instantaneous and diffuse, rather than cumulative, cultivated in relation to the fact that videos are rarely shown in their entireties. Embodied and literalistic line delivery is uncommon nowadays and the 'acting out' of songs is considered outmoded and distinctly tacky in comparison to the creation of a graspable persona which could plausibly span beyond and across a range of songs or life-style posturings.

However, these marked distinctions between music video delivery style and acting do not bode well for crossover artists hoping to segue between two worlds without significantly altering their means of expression. One suitable example (and there are plenty to chose from) exists in *Freejack* (Murphy, 1992), a film in which Mick Jagger hardly bristles with Satanic majesty as the villain Vacendak.[9] Granted, the film's lack of critical and audience acclaim could easily be equally attributable to a lack-lustre performance from co-star Emilio Estevez and an uninspired script, editing, direction and so on, but Jagger's reluctance or inability to bow down to the working conventions of acting, as well as his commitment to the rules of pop stardom, hammer many nails into the film's coffin.

One thing that betrays his 'bad acting' is the fact that his accent slips and slides across the Atlantic (very rarely do natives of Kent say 'asshole' without the English 'r' as a second letter). Inaccurate accents are high on the check list of how to spot inadequate realist acting: Keanu Reeves fell foul as an unconvincing Englishman in *Bram Stoker's Dracula* (Coppola, 1992), whilst, at her peak, Meryl

Streep gained much praise for her acute sense of hearing and vocal precision. However, the mid-Atlantic accent does uphold conventions of pop delivery. It is particularly common for British pop musicians to sing in American accents, a tradition which Jagger himself helped to establish, and which is another definite, if not deliberate, throwback to his pop identity. Likewise, his over-emphatic diction throughout *Freejack* (and many of his other films) is somewhat misplaced and distinctly more suited to the projection techniques which are vital to performing in stadia.

Jagger's unwavering stares and almost pantomimic movements recall the sorts of images that music videos require. Yet without the necessary editing rhythms to chop up and vary such pose-striking, a more sustained camera gaze gives Jagger's acting an unsubtle, hammy quality unsuited to the diversity and progression of a film's narrative. Perhaps the most grating of these gestures is an eagerly repeated pouting mouth which is simultaneously too crass a facial shape to comply with the rules of big screen acting, and also the most obvious marker of 'Mick Jagger' possible. If at any point we were to forget we were watching Mick Jagger, then Jerry Hall is on hand to provide a knowing cameo as a TV presenter.

Extra-textual references like these are, of course, widespread in film acting of all types and, where musician-actors are concerned, they can often be woven into a narrative to great effect. Madonna's re-enactment and expansion of her self-sufficient bohemian persona in *Desperately Seeking Susan* (Seidelman, 1985) harmed neither the film's story-line nor her subsequent musical career, and Courtney Love's role in *The People vs. Larry Flint* (Foreman, 1996) successfully coalesced her 'out on a limb' public image with the part of a drug-using, free-speech advocating pornographic pin-up. Jagger himself is similarly complemented within *Performance* (Roeg and Cammell, 1970), a movie which builds upon a pre-established notion of 'Jagger' rather than situating so unadaptable an entity in an utterly foreign filmic world. The balance, however, is a delicate one, as Yvonne Tasker concludes in relation to Madonna's acting in *Body of Evidence* (Edel, 1992):

> [the film is] unsatisfactory since, in contrast to Madonna as 'vamp' in countless music videos or live performances, she is situated as manipulative and devious before being killed off. It is not so much that something is 'lost' in the transition between media, but that there is no easy fit or equivalence between the narrative cinema and the evocative 'narrative' images associated with the musical star.[10]

The same could easily be said of Jagger's acting in *Freejack*: whilst he is evidently an attraction of the film, he seems to trample over all the other potential draws, the intricacies that make films 'work'. Star quality clashes with convincing narrative realism, swamping the team effort so crucial to enjoyable cinema (especially when a lead figure is unconvincing) in favour of overwhelming – possibly egotistical – self-promotion. Here the strong and relentless notion of individualism so prized in musical stardom is a distinct disadvantage.

In his *Sight and Sound* review of *Freejack* Mark Kermode remarks upon Jagger's 'unintentionally hilarious performance'[11] – something which highlights the star's hubris, his inability to see the limitations of his skills. The key word here, the one which delights so many mockers of musicians' bad acting, is unintentional: it highlights the very fallibility which stars are supposed not to show in the work-place. In much fan and celebrity discourse there is an emphasis on stars having 'it', that indefinable quality which makes them universally marvellous. When both acting and musicianship hold particularly ambiguous places in the taxonomies of labour value and, indeed, in what constitutes their labour in the first place, much store is placed in less explainable qualities such as charisma. Unlike classical musicianship or Shakespearean acting, say, there is much less quantifiable training and qualification written into the meritocracies of film or popular music performance. Whilst this opens up windows of hope for wannabes, it also leaves the professions hopelessly exposed to claims that their labour is worthless – hence the heavy stock placed in magically intangible get-out clauses like charisma. What is so upsetting about Jagger's inability to win his audience in *Freejack* is that his supposedly abundant and dependable charisma is seen to be in shorter reserves than we imagined. His charisma does not grant him indefinite immunity to mucking in with the work of acting, to getting his hands dirty. The total absorption and seeming effortlessness that esteemed acting performances display is treasured all the more when we see musicians trying so hard to convince us with their cinematic characterisations (and the same is true of actors who wrongly consider themselves to be plausible singers). Yet, we are still unsure where precisely the magic comes from and here we run into a complex interweave of beliefs about 'natural talent' and 'hard work' which, as the affluent western economies continue to shift their focus from manual to cultural industry, seem decidedly difficult to pin down. Interestingly, Richard Dyer (1979) defines charisma as a quality which bridges points which have been polarised by historical instabilities and this perspective may well shed light on how shifts in working patterns are debated symbolically through our engagement with celebrity culture. As a 1960s icon, Jagger successfully encapsulated the libertarian indolence and raw working stamina that marked the two extremes of the post-war economic boom and its relationship with philosophies and practices of labour. Unfortunately, though, he seems not to have managed to bring together similarly opposing forces in his acting duties in *Freejack*.

But why are we so keen to lampoon such non-standard work? In an age when we are encouraged to shift from job to job, to glorify the ability to 'multi-task' in response to increased insecurity and casualisation in the work-place, this disgust at someone branching out is telling. Both acting and musicianship are, and almost always have been, freelance jobs *par excellence*; contracts are short and easily legally terminated. However, they are highly desirable careers and the rickety nature of any given performer's staying power simultaneously seems to offer up opportunities for new talent waiting in the wings. As Peters and Cantor point out, the standards by which acting competence are judged are hazy, meaning that the scope to fantasize one's suitability for the job is surprisingly broad:

> For them [actors], power in the workplace is not based on skill or knowledge, nor has a meritocracy developed… the criterion is nebulous and, in fact, is considered undefinable [sic] even by the agents, casting directors, and producers who apply it. Still, there is always the possibility for a person to begin with virtually no capital or credentials and to become eminently successful. It is this feature of the occupation which probably explains the remarkable persistence of many aspiring actors in the face of deprivation and compromise. It is also this feature of the occupation which makes most actors powerless to control their own work lives.[12]

This situation embodies what McRobbie (2002) terms a lottery economy. Whilst there is fabulous wealth for the few, and uncertainty, financial worry and drudge for the vast majority, the glamorous existence one could *potentially* gain makes the dream worth chasing.[13]

Yet, this hope, this faith placed in the seemingly egalitarian factors of both professions is grossly undermined when we see stars shifting effortlessly from one art form to another. Here 'multi-tasking' is not backed up with an adequate 'multi-skilled portfolio' and the more undesirable sides of wafting between jobs – including the nepotism and prejudice one will probably encounter – becomes blatantly obvious. When we consider how scarce these coveted jobs are, the jumped-up outsider, the greedy yuppie crossover performer, is even less welcome, however much they fulfill another department's star criteria. At the expense of other hopefuls, the already rich are getting richer.

Perhaps most grating is the fact that large amounts of money are shovelled into the hands of people who we have problems pinning exact value on. Whilst star mythology has regularly presented the idea that actors and musicians work for and are driven by a pure love of their art, the material gains of fame are also absolutely integral to our attraction to and irritation with the famous. And these elements map themselves very clearly onto the politicised semantics of work and leisure, a matrix within which performers must profitably position themselves. A Robert de Niro or a Bruce Springsteen, for instance, make their toiling as noticeable as possible, upholding a belief that money must be *earned*, preferably through a good measure of physical exertion. Then there are performers who take on outside activities, such as the promotion of charities or political causes – work that can also be seen as multi-layered investment. Such commitments to manual or moral labour are eschewed by the other stars who cultivate fabulous idleness (at least in their leisure time) and a willingness to delegate the simplest of chores (eye-brow plucking, for instance) to swarms of employees. It is unusual, even enviable, activities like these that are crucial for the maintenance of our (financially exploitable) inquisitiveness about and even political acceptance of such stars' incomes. The public's insatiability for monitoring each star's worth in terms of their deserved or unwarranted decadence highlights not only the tenuous connections between luck, talent and hard work, but also how much, in an unpredictable work climate, many of us long for more exacting modes of categorising 'work'.

Ultimately, perhaps, pop singers who 'can't act' help justify the salaries of big name movie stars, making it clear who does and does not deserve film stardom, bringing issues of effort and professionalism to the fore whilst other areas of the industry try and efface them. This is not to say that rock stars are a cheap casting option, but that, unwittingly or not, when we take lurid fascination in their sub-standard work, we are trying to create a rather conservative value system by enforcing a particular division of labour in an arena where talent fluctuates, job criteria cannot be pinned down and ultimate worth is indistinct. When musicians are incompetent within films and actors who try to launch singing careers flop, does this help reinforce a more comforting and explainable set of job descriptions (although, ultimately, it is doubtful that we would want such vocations demystified in every sense)? We encourage fixity within this troublingly awkward terrain to such an extent that substantial profits can be made from our need to simultaneously ridicule and reaffirm through indulgence in a 'so bad it's good' night out at the cinema. We are also paying for the privilege of *judging*, of assessing the potential for worthwhile craftsmanship.

With all this potential animosity towards the crossover star lurking around the nearest corner, it seems strange that multi-national corporations are still so willing to cast singers in films (recently, for instance, Britney Spears has appeared in *Crossroads* (Davis, 2002) and Charlotte Church in *I'll Be There* (Ferguson, 2003)). After all, with the widespread horizontal integration of the entertainment industries, companies can rely on, as they frequently do, profits and cross-promotion from compilation soundtracks. It is possible, after all, to entice a Celine Dion fan to *Titanic* (Cameron, 1997) without having to replace Kate Winslet with her. However, although these are popular strategies in the entertainment industries, they do block certain elements of a singing star's pulling power. The first is the *sense of occasion* that is created when a star crosses over, something that is all-important in the age of the event movie. Whether or not the musician produces labour of quality, the work does much to bring the star into public prominence and, seemingly, this is a gamble worth taking. Then there is the respect for entrepreneurial drive that is currently generated by many crossover stars – ironically, because the quantity of work being done seems to be greater than that of other performers.

Jennifer Lopez – or rather the all-conquering 'brand' J-Lo – epitomises this trend, stamping her recognisable star presence onto a range of products which are consequently more easily imprinted on the buyers' memories. J-Lo marches from platform to platform (films, music, clothes…) so indefatigably that her energy and determination mark her out as a paragon of two central and respected ways of conceptualising labour (at least in the US): 'the Protestant work ethic' and 'the American dream' (around which her vacillating performance of 'race' is intriguing). However, whilst she scores points for the amount of work she completes, faults have been found in the quality of her end products. Her singing, in particular, has run up against critical derision and is generally regarded as 'weaker' than the acting skills which first brought her into the limelight.

Yet, by crossing over from film to music, she seems less crippled by her perceived limitations than Mick Jagger, who has made the move in the opposite direction. The music industry operates with an arsenal of corrective technologies (such as filters and pitch correctors) which mean an artist need not necessarily have a 'perfect' singing voice.[14] It is also acceptable practice to perform live by miming to play-back recordings, although, if one wishes to be respected as an Artist, this is not advisable. As I suggested earlier, though, music culture places great stock in authenticity – so much so that, whilst most would acknowledge J-Lo's current popularity, it is doubtful that she will be remembered as a Great Singer. Those suspicious of J-Lo's appeal can then put her fame down to such things as marketing, hype and backstage manipulation – work done by others which somewhat undermines belief in her laudable individual effort.

So, even in relation to successful examples like J-Lo's crossover career/self-commodification, we still have a fervent desire to establish some rules and meritocracies for assessing the prominent media industries. Such yardsticks must not only cater for the work done at the more moneyed end of the scale, but should also help others positioned less profitably within the west's decreasingly blue collar economies to gauge their working worth (and this would also include the world's legions of manual labourers). The currently favoured balance is a complex one: we seem to want the accessibility of wealth with which a 'lottery economy' tempts us, yet we often cannot abide those who do not 'deserve' their affluence. Until we can agree on how to actually value and reward work (which seems almost entirely impossible under the strategic and globally inconsistent fluctuations of contemporary capitalism), then the over-indulgences and failures of the stars this system offers us will continue to fascinate us. Moreover, this situation provides us with more of a forum for critiquing our working frameworks than we are encouraged to imagine.

Notes

1. Richard Benson in 'Culture' section of *The Independent on Sunday*, 28 May 2000, p3.
2. Thomas Quinn in 'The "A" List' supplement, *The Mirror*, 28 May 2000, p5.
3. These are the kinds of much welcome debates which are brought into the study of film stardom (an area that has traditionally been theorised in terms of structuralism and semiotics) by Barry King, 'Articulating Stardom' in *Screen*, Vol. 26 No. 5, 1985, pp27-50; Jane M. Gaines, *Contested Culture: The Image, the Voice and the Law*, BFI Publishing, London 1992 and Danae Clark, *Negotiating Hollywood: The Cultural Politics of Actors' Labor*, University of Minesota Press, Minneapolis 1995.
4. Clark, op cit, p19.
5. Richard Dyer, *Stars*, BFI Publishing, London 1979.
6. Paul McDonald, 'Film Acting' in J. Hill and P. Church Gibson (eds), *The Oxford Guide to Film Studies*, Oxford University Press, Oxford 1998, p34.
7. David Thompson, 'Pop and Film: The Charisma Crossover' in Jonathan Romney and Adrian Wooton (eds), *Celluloid Jukebox: Popular Music and the Movies Since the 50s*, BFI Publishing, London 1995, p34.
8. Angela McRobbie, 'From Holloway to Hollywood: Happiness at Work in the New Cultural Economy' in Paul du Gay and Michael Pryke (eds), *Cultural Economy, Cultural Analysis and Commercial Life*, Sage, London 2002, p99.
9. Rather ironically, *Freejack*'s script is an attack on multi-national corporations, precisely the entities which are most responsible for suggesting that stars cross over in the first place.
10. Yvonne Tasker, *Working Girls: Gender and Sexuality in Popular Cinema*, Routledge, London 1998, p183.
11. Mark Kermode, 'Freejack' in *Sight and Sound*, October 1992, p66.
12. Peters, A. and Cantor, M., 'Screen Acting as Work' in James Ettema and D.C. Whitney (eds), *Individuals in Mass Communication Organizations*, Sage, Beverly Hills 1982, p65.
13. This situation can also be extremely detrimental to the struggle for workers' rights within the entertainment industries. The huge amounts of aspirants guarantee that some hopefuls will be willing to undercut others in a variety of ways (including submitting to the 'casting couch'), something which places the inscription of acceptable working conditions squarely in the upper hands of the employers. Likewise, successful performers are kept in line by the fear that they might easily be superseded by a newcomer if they fall out of favour with their bosses.
14. Of course film works in these ways too – there is post-production vocal dubbing and the possibility of using body doubles, for example. However, I would argue that these are more peripheral clean-up devices than the ones used so regularly in the music business.

Small faces

The tyranny of celebrity in post-Oedipal culture

Jeremy Gilbert

Recent decades have seen the proliferation of cultural formations whose main substance is discourse on 'celebrities'. Commentary – academic and otherwise – on this phenomenon is always informed by assumptions about the nature of the relationship between social life and individuality. While the conventional psychoanalytic account of the relationship between stars and their fans reproduce the assumptions of early 20th century mass psychology, assumptions also reproduced by much neo-Lacanian political theory, these assumptions are challenged by a range of theoretical and empirical sources, from studies of the cultural productivity of 'fans' to the deconstructions of psychoanalysis offered by Deleuze and Guattari and Mikkel Borch-Jacobsen. Taken together, these different formulations can all be used to produce an account of celebrity culture as inherent to capitalism from the moment of its earliest emergence, and symptomatic of the fundamental incompatibility between capitalist individualism and any form of meaningful democracy.

> 'Even the greatest stars
> Discover themselves in the looking glass'
> *Kraftwerk*

The face and the crowd: the politics of recognition

In these star-struck times, 'the celebrity' is a key site at which the meaning and nature of contemporary individuality are struggled over. Thinking about celebrity, as P. David Marshall shows,[1] is always informed by general sets of assumptions on the nature of individuality and sociality. For example, the assumption that the masses are simply dazzled by the glamour which Hollywood can lend to the mythic individuals it creates has its roots in the early 20th century social psychology of Le Bon and Tarde, implying as it does that at root all collectivities will tend towards the mindlessness of fascism. In fact, one of the questions to be addressed here will be that of whether it is possible to observe the rise and rise of celebrity culture without concluding that humanity in general is cursed with a weakness for the charisma of strong leaders. Firstly, however, I want to address a crucial question: what do we *mean* when we use the word 'celebrity'?

'A Celebrity'; 'A Personality': these two near-synonymous terms are almost unique in contemporary English usage. In either case, a word is used which designates both a general abstraction and a particular instance of that abstraction concretised in the person of a named individual. 'Celebrity' is that which a celebrity possesses. A celebrity is an instance of celebrity. A personality is known not for thoughts or deeds, but for personality. In either case both the distinction between having and being and that between the universal and the particular are semantically erased: celebrities /personalities both have and are celebrity/personality. What's more, in either case a universal quality which can only ever pertain to individuals is what is designated as being particularly instantiated in the named example. Celebrities are individualities: individuals who are more individual (more distinct, more noteworthy) than other individuals. Personalities have more of what makes us all who we are than we do. If nothing else, this linguistic oddity ought to alert us to the need for some rigorous yet very general thought about what a term like 'celebrity' actually means.

What, then, is a celebrity? There are many possible answers to the question, but this is surely the most basic, the most fundamental, and the most irreducible: a celebrity is someone who is recognised by more people than they themselves recognise. To be more specific, we might posit that a celebrity is someone whose *face* is widely recognised. Surely there have been, since ancient times, persons famous for writing, for speaking, for governing, for fighting, for playing and/or composing music; but I would suggest that it is only at the point where the physical visages of such individuals have been subject to practices of public display and/or reproduction, which make them familiar to a public beyond that of their acquaintance, that they have ever become 'celebrities' in the sense that we use the term today. 1960s mod slang – which called any well-recognised individual a 'face' – is only the purest expression of this general principle.

It's easy to forget that the mass reproduction of images did not begin with the invention of photography, or lithography, or print. In fact, the earliest example of the image of a face entering into mass production is the coinage of the ancient world. Around 300 BC Ptolemy of Egypt minted the first coin to bear a likeness of a living ruler, not long after a Macedonian coin bearing the likeness of the deified Alexander the Great had become the first coin to depict a mortal at all, and this must rank as one of the first examples of celebrity as we know it being produced.[2] It would be foolish to understate the differences between the function of charismatic authority in a primitive imperial theocracy and in contemporary cultures of fame. However, it would be equally foolish to ignore the significance of this observation – that the mass reproduction of faces begins at the moment when an ancient despotism institutionalises the most fundamental mechanism of commodity exchange: currency. The face-which-is-recognised is the very medium of capitalist relations. But what does such recognition consist of? Why does it happen? How does it work?

The concept of recognition has been in some ways central to political philosophy since the beginning of the nineteenth century. Hegel's most famous illustration of the dialectic is his account of the 'struggle for recognition'[3] between master and slave, wherein the master finds himself dependent on the recognition of the slave for his authority, such that that his own status as a fully self-conscious being is revealed as arguably inferior to that of the slave. The slave's sense of self, unlike that of the master, is constituted by the full experience of negativity – in the form of servitude and the real threat of death to which the master subjects him – and the experience of work as agency.[4] Many different interpretations of this scenario and its significance have been offered, but what is clear is that Hegel sees a certain *mutual* recognition as constitutive of human being and self-consciousness. How might this relate to the situation of celebrity culture? Well, such a perspective could map quite neatly onto a particular position which can be taken with regard to forms of mass-mediated popular culture which revolve around the production and circulation of celebrities. Such a perspective would point out the extent to which celebrity is always in the gift of the audience: celebrities of stage, screen, record or dispatch box rise and fall according to their popularity with the public. The celebrity is only ever a product of the desires and fantasies of their fans. According to this scenario, the secret truth of celebrity culture is that all of the power lies with the anonymous public of whose fantasies and whims the career of the celebrity is merely an index.

This view is one which could draw implicit support from a range of sources. In particular it would chime well with that optimistic line of thought which includes the 'uses and gratifications' school of post-war media research and the 'cultural populism' of John Fiske. Fiske notoriously understands late modern media culture as a 'semiotic democracy',[5] in which the individuals and groups who consume media products do so in their own ways, attributing meanings to texts and events with very little regard to the apparent intentions of authors and producers, or for the ideological messages encoded in such texts. Such work, especially that of Fiske, has come in for an enormous amount of criticism over the years, especially within the cultural studies tradition. The frequency and vehemence of attacks on Fiske's ideas, out of all proportion to their importance or influence, and in general decidedly unnecessarily ungenerous towards Fiske's clearly heartfelt radical politics, say more about the lack of imagination displayed by his attackers than they do about his ideas or anyone else's.[6] On the other hand, the complicity of such a view with neo-liberal ideology – which claims before anything else that the free market is the very model of functional democracy, delivering what the people want, when they want it – should always make us suspicious. However, it is not necessary to take such an optimistic view of matters to agree with Marshall that 'the celebrity's strength or power as a discourse on the individual is operationalized only in terms of the power and position of the audience that has allowed it to circulate.'[7] It is clearly true that to an extent the success of any given celebrity is dependent on the goodwill of her fans. At the same time Alexander Garcia Düttmann's reflections on the ambiguities inherent in the very concept of recognition offer some useful and relevant insights. As Düttmann points out, recognition is never simply recognition, and never wholly something else. Recognition always acts in part, performatively, to posit that which it 'recognises', yet to 'recognise' is never simply to create. The object which is recognised is never simply an inert object, reflected in the mirror of consciousness, or a simple effect of the act of recognition. It is neither cognition nor creation. Hence the relationship between celebrity and public must be never simple, but never simply dialectical.

This might not seem to get us much further than Marshall's observation that celebrity culture is a site of discursive struggle, but it does at least illustrate a dimension of celebrity culture which must always be kept in mind when trying to comment on it: that struggle for recognition which characterises the relationship between the celebrity and her audience is always riven with ambiguities and tensions. The relationship cannot simply be seen in terms of a one-way mirror, the audience gazing at the star while the star sees nothing but their own glory reflected. The celebrity is always watching the audience at least as closely as they are watching her, even if the nature and means of that 'watching' differ (checking the TV ratings, the chart positions, the reactions in the street…). As Chris Rojek puts it: 'despite external appearances, celebrities are perhaps the most insecure of people'.[8]

But why? Why do those who seek and those who remain merely fascinated by celebrity and its instantiations persist in these exchanges of empty regard? Rojek suggests that: 'public acclaim answers to a deep psychological need in all of us for recognition. Acclaim carries the sensual pleasure of being acknowledged as an object of desire and approval.'[9] Relating the rise of a culture of celebrity to the decline of religion (a core symptom and feature of Western modernity), Rojek writes that 'the desire to be recognised as special or unique is perhaps an inevitable feature of cultures built around an ethic of individualism'.[10] One might add to this the observation that the desire *to recognise* is also a symptom of the historical breakdown of stable forms of community, imagined or otherwise. One of the noted features of modern life, as distinct from life in traditional societies, is the constant presence of strangers and the lack of intimate knowledge of those with whom we share spaces and flows. Simmel famously writes of the experience of the modern metropolis as characterised by the 'blasé attitude' towards others necessitated by this feature of modern existence.[11] In this sense, the existence of public figures about whom much is known, and who retain a certain visual familiarity, might be seen as answering to a human need to recognise, to find anchoring points in a sea of anonymous strangers, as well as being symptomatic of a culture in which knowledge of other individuals is increasingly at a premium (isn't this what marketing firms, dating agencies, a whole range of state institutions, are all paid to produce, provide and act on?).

There can be little question that individualisation is the dominant social process of our time. This is certainly the view of commentators such as Beck/Beck-Gernsheim[12] and Bauman.[13] The relentless implementation of market relations by the agents and institutions of neo-liberal capitalism increasingly renders unsustainable any form of meaningful collectivity. Under such circumstances, the personalisation of social relations and the tendency to make collective points of identification out of the super-individuals we call 'celebrities' are well-documented. The complexities of this situation, riven by the ambiguities which Düttmann identifies as typical of any recognition-situation, in part illustrate and are in part symptomatic of the paradoxical effects of this process. The dissolution of all established collectivities is invariably legitimated in terms of the need to liberate the individual from constrictive social ties – to place, nation, kin, class, church, or even company – and yet 'the individual' is itself threatened by such liberation insofar as it only ever acquires its identity on the basis of *belonging* to one or more such communities. The 'I' who is part of no 'we' whatsoever has no position from which to speak, and tends to experience the dissolution of stable communitarian ties in terms of the postmodern 'schizophrenia'[14] of fragmented belonging, experiencing herself not as individual at all, but as increasingly divided. Under such circumstances, it seems almost inevitable that people will cling to those points of common identification which are the least incompatible with the prevailing ideology of individualism. While loyalty to nationalism, socialism, religion and even more localised or dispersed sites of collective identification (football clubs, music cultures, hobby networks) is always vulnerable to being undermined by the relentlessly disaggregating force of individualisation,[15] the celebrity-discourse – a discursive formation which simply takes the form of an individual's public biography and a collection of commentary on it – is always already fully imbricated with the discourse of competitive individualism. One might even speak here of 'celebritism' as that implicit epistemology which regards the publicly mediated mythic lives of famous individuals as the basis for accepted knowledge on what it can mean to be a person. Within this context celebrities function as meta-individuals: 'tendentially empty signifiers'[16] which stand for the possibility of individuality as such while also offering concrete examples of its successful particularisation.

Psychoanalytic reflections

Rojek's comments here – and some of mine – are implicitly informed by the standard psychoanalytic account of the psychic relationship between celebrities and their public. Just as the infant sees in her reflection an image of autonomous and self-contained integrity, so different from the state of confusion which she experiences as herself, so the fan sees in the star an image of perfect autonomy, public agency, smooth-edged self-completion. Lacan famously describes this phantasmatic relationship of subject to reflection as a *misrecognition*.[17]

Celebrities in the public domain, according to such a view, function as fantasy objects, images of impossible perfection which hold out the lure of a fully-achieved selfhood to subjects constituted by their perpetual search for just such impossible/absent 'fullness'.[18] Despite the currency of this received account, it actually raises more questions than it answers. Is this simply an inevitable feature of psychic and social life? Doesn't psychoanalysis teach us that all mental life is constituted by such fantasies, and that all social life is only made possible by them? In certain respects it does. Identification with the 'ideal ego' is certainly necessary to the formation of subjectivity according to the Freudian schema.[19] What's more, collectivities as described by Freud and his followers down to the present day are invariably produced by means of a common (but not exactly shared) identification of the members of the collectivity with a single figure of authority or a symbol which plays an identical role.

In Slavoj Zizek's neo-Lacanian terms, the rise of celebrity culture might be one symptom of the decline of the 'big Other': the stable symbolic system of publicly accepted social norms and values, and the institutions and agencies thought to authorise and be authorised by it. The breakdown of established communities of meaning and the rise of 'reflexive modernity'[20] creates a situation in which subjects desperately seek out a plethora of substitutes for these passing structures. One of Zizek's examples is the proliferation of public committees established to resolve discrete ethical questions (on the correct use of genetic technology, for example) which can no longer be resolved in terms of an overall ethical schema. 'It is as if the lack of the big Other is supplanted by so many "small big Others" on to which the subject transposes his responsibility and from which he expects to receive formula which will resolve his deadlock.'[21] Zizek immediately relates this situation to the decline of symbolic paternal authority (a phenomenon documented empirically by Castells as 'the end of patriarchalism'[22]):

> Today...a father is no longer perceived as one's *Ego-Ideal*, the (more or less failed, inadequate) bearer of symbolic authority, but as one's *ideal ego*, imaginary competitor – with the result that subjects never really 'grow up', that we are dealing with individuals in their thirties and forties who remain, in

terms of their psychic economy, 'immature' adolescents competing with their fathers.[23]

The expansion of celebrity culture can clearly be understood in these terms. The celebrity may be a 'role model', but is rarely if ever such in the traditional sense of a full ethical template which a lesser individual can in all good conscience seek to emulate in every regard. Rather, celebrities represent points on an imaginary scale of achievement, always deliberately two-dimensional, partial images of success. In Zizek's terms, we should no doubt relate the imaginary function of the celebrity to the function of the obscene Imaginary father who 'enjoins us to enjoy', the Super-Ego whose secret message is not that of the moral law which prohibits enjoyment, but of an endless imperative to break all communitarian prohibitions in the pursuit of an enjoyment which can never be sufficient to satisfy it.[24] The celebrity almost by definition is depicted as engaging in conspicuous, hedonistic consumption, a perpetual exhortation to the audience to seek a life of luxury which they can never achieve: or, more precisely, to make such a life the main substance of the fantasies which organise their relation to the world (it would be ridiculously crude to say that any but a handful of those who 'dream of living like the stars' actually *want* that life in any effective sense, insofar as such wanting would involve a relentless pursuit for which in most cases the fantasy itself is a preferred substitute).

Through the looking-glass: a social-ist deconstruction of celebrity culture

As powerful as they are, what such psychoanalytic accounts leave out is any real engagement with that phenomenon of recognition understood as relational but not dialectical. While they may explain some features of celebrity culture as we know it, and some of the reasons for its appeal for certain publics, it ultimately offers us insight into these phenomena only from the point of the view of the viewing subject for whom the celebrity is a particular type of fantasy object. Given our earlier observations, in particular those following Düttmann, this is surely inadequate: what we need in addition is not simply some way of seeing things 'from the celebrities' point of view', but a way of taking account of the dynamics of the relationships between the various participants in celebrity culture. The inability of a straightforwardly psychoanalytic account to engage with such dynamics is telling, but not surprising. In fact, the account of human sociality on which all such psychoanalytic explanations rests is deeply problematic, in ways which have a direct bearing on our topic here. Freud's social psychology was directly derived from the work of Le Bon, and, as Marshall shows, it was this model of how human beings relate to each other collectively which informed most early pronouncements about the nature and function of celebrity in modern culture.[25] Freud's re-working of Le Bon provides a model according to which any collectivity is bound together by the common identification of its members with a single leader. This idea remains powerful in contemporary political theory. According to Renata Salecl, a colleague of Zizek's, 'the sad conclusion one can draw from this is that some kind of master is always in place regardless of how much we deny its existence'.[26] Drawing most directly on Lacan's account of the function of the phallus as the empty guarantee of the consistency of the symbolic order, but also inheriting the emphases and implicit conclusions of Freud's social psychology, Ernesto Laclau's recent work stresses the centrality of 'tendentially empty signifiers' to political discourse. What all such work tends to imply, or in the case of Salecl to make explicit, is the view that it is the more-or-less arbitrary identification of a collection of individuals with a single central figure, leader, image, or term (be it the Pope, 'America' or 'Socialism') which sustains the existence of any form of collectivity or community whatsoever.

This model can be criticised from a number of points of view. The most precise critique to date has been that offered by Mikkel Borch-Jacobsen in his deconstruction of Freud's social psychology, *The Freudian Subject*. Borch-Jacobsen painstakingly demonstrates the lengths to which Freud goes to insist that the collective identity of group members is entirely dependent on each making a discrete individual identification with a singular leader: a leader who, like the father of the primal horde, is himself apparently fully autonomous, not even subject to that dialectical dependency on his followers' recognition which characterises the position of the Hegelian Master. The irreducibility of 'the master' to all forms of society, an irreducibility which Salecl sees as inherent in this model of sociality (a model to which she subscribes), is clearly dependent on this assumed understanding of human collectivity, an understanding which refuses any possibility of experiences and identifications which might be genuinely *shared* rather than merely replicated amongst the members of the group. For Borch-Jacobsen, the affective force of *suggestion* which can circulate, for better or worse, between members of a crowd, between a therapist and a patient, etc, is a form of lateral 'mimetic identification' between members of a group which is analytically distinct from their private individual identifications with any central locus of power and meaning.

This is clearly related to Deleuze and Guattari's insistence on the significance of the transversal relations between members of groups. In a number of ways, Deleuze and Guattari insist on the importance of understanding the relationships between members of groups as at least potentially lateral and horizontal in nature. For example, in their discussion of the micro-politics of music they introduce the term '*Dividual*, to designate the type of musical relations and the intra- or intergroup passages occurring in group individuation'.[27] Their famous distinction between rhizomatic and arborescent systems, which contrasts the decentred, networked horizontality of the former to the structured, vertical hierarchy of the latter, similarly implies the necessary possibility of polyvalent lateral connection between different components of any collectivity. This is not to say that Deleuze and Guattari deny the existence of 'psychic formations'[28] of which those described in psychoanalytic literature would be typical, but only to point out that such formations do not exhaust the possibilities of human experience. This is made clear in their distinction between such 'subjugated groups' and 'subject groups':

> Every investment is collective, every fantasy is a group fantasy and in this sense a position of reality. But the two kinds of investments are radically different, according as the one bears upon the molar structures that subordinate the molecules, and the other on the contrary bears upon the molecular multiplicities that subordinate the structured crowd phenomena. One is a *subjugated* group investment, as much in its sovereign forms as in its colonial formations of the gregarious aggregate, which socially and psychically represses the desire of persons; the other, a *subject-group* investment in the transverse multiplicities that convey desire as a molecular phenomenon, that is, as partial objects, and flows, as opposed to aggregates and persons.[29]

This depiction of group fantasy sustained by 'transverse multiplicities' has a profound resonance with some recent research into celebrity culture. For some considerable time now, the semiotic activity of publics, in particular of fans of particular types of media product (including individual celebrities), has been an object of investigation for researchers from a variety of perspectives. The fact that in general fan cultures are sustained by the exchange of opinions and ideas, of feelings and fantasies, *between* members of a cultural network might itself be understood as evidence of the importance of this transversal dimension to actually identifiable cultural formations.

It might be thought that the formations to which this description could most accurately be applied are those to which the persistence of 'celebrity' is the least important. The idea of fandom as an 'interpretive community' is most vividly illustrated by those formations characterised by the presence of horizontal networks for the circulation of 'fan fictions', but in such formations it tends to be the fictional narratives and the characters who populate them – The Doctor, Buffy the Vampire Slayer, Captain Kirk, etc – which are the focus of attention and identification, rather than the celebrity actors whose lives and work outside the particular relevant screen role are of notoriously little interest to most fans. However, there is more than one reason to be sceptical about the utility of making a clear distinction between such formations.

It might be argued, for example, that even those celebrity cultures which are clearly focussed on the lives and personae of actual living (or recently living) individuals – Princess Diana, for example – are characterised by the constant circulation, modification and exchange of narratives. From those forms of 'gossip' and fantasy which never reach the printed page, to the deliberately fictionalised accounts circulated or deliberately implied by the reporting of the broadcast and print media, to the production of actual narrative fictions, the circulation of partially-authored narratives sustains the formation in question.

Crucially, what is involved in all such cases is a transversal exchange of meanings and affects not reducible to a simple identification with the nominal focal figure. The example of Princess Diana and her following illustrates some of these points usefully. What relatively few of the commentators on the massive public reaction to the death of Diana noted was the power of this collective, *horizontal* dynamic in assembling huge crowds in demonstrations of collective mourning. Almost all commentary focussed on the question of what Diana had *meant* (i.e. what Diana had signified, how she had functioned as a point of identification) to the *individuals* making up the crowds,[30] but relatively little attention was paid to the power of the crowds themselves to constitute an affective assemblage which had little purpose or meaning beyond its own existence; to the power of a certain non-signifiable affectivity to bring together such numbers of people, drawn to *each other* as much as to Diana the Princess or Diana the everygirl. Of course, that commentary which decried the irrationality of such behaviour was entirely couched in terms of a Le Bonian crowd psychology, which sees the 'contagious' nature of such collective affects as inherently dangerous, irresponsible and deplorable. However, the simple dignity displayed by the crowds which so assembled, whatever one may think of the implicit politics of their veneration of Diana, itself completely undermines the characterisation of such affective crowds on which Freud's entire account of social psychology rests.

Of course no adequate account of the dynamics of celebrity culture could overlook the question of the nature of the psychic relationship of individual fans to their celebrity icons. Here again, however, the theoretical framework offered by Mikkel Borch-Jacobsen provides a uniquely neat solution to some recently identified analytical problems. Matt Hills's recent study *Fan Cultures* points out the philosophical and methodological difficulties inherent in attempting to map the psychosocial processes involved in practices of celebrity impersonation and the cultures within which they are located. Hills introduces into his sophisticated neo-Winicottian object-relations schema (wherein fan cultures are seen to emerge around texts to the extent that those texts become specific types of 'transitional object' for certain individuals) the notion of 'performative consumption', to explain the ambivalence inherent in the practices of celebrity imitation, of which Elvis-impersonators are the most numerous practitioners.

> Performative consumption enacts the dialectic at the heart of the fan cult(ure). It is simultaneously a matter of communal and cultural 'exchange value' and a matter of intensely private or cultic 'use value'...

> I have also argued that performative consumption is a useful term because it refers to the oscillation between intense 'self-reflexivity' and 'self absence' which is typical of fan cult(ure)s...
>
> By blurring the lines between self and other, fan impersonation challenges cultural norms of the fixed and bounded self. Criticisms of fan impersonation tend to be produced within 'common sense' notions of 'good' voluntarist individualism, therefore dismissing fan-impersonators as lacking a 'strong-enough' self-identity.[31]

This situation might usefully be theorised in terms of Borch-Jacobsen and Renée Girard's notion of 'mimetic desire'. From the point of view of Borch-Jacobsen and Girard, the 'common sense' which Hills criticises is central in shaping the Freudian account of identity-formation upon which all psychoanalysis ultimately rests. From their perspective, such individualism is inherent in the insistence on maintaining that clear topological distinction between identification and desire on which Freud's entire Oedipal narrative depends: Freud's male child assumes individuality and masculinity precisely in identifying with that parent whom he does not desire and who blocks his desire: the father. Borch-Jacobsen's and Girard's radical move beyond such a conception is to understand desire itself as inherently mimetic in character. Developing Girard's account of desire as proceeding from a mimetic identification – in other words, we desire that which our model seems to desire, rather than simply identifying with that-with-which-we-do-not-desire[32]– Borch-Jacobsen posits an originary mimesis-desire as the basic mechanism of identification which makes subjectivity possible while foreclosing any possibility of full self-identity.[33] Understood in these terms, the emulation of our idols (be they Elvis Presley or our mums and dads) is not only non-pathological, it is in fact precisely the mechanism by which all subjectivity is acquired in the first place.

What is crucial for our discussion here is Borch-Jacobsen's persuasive insistence that mimesis-desire is also indistinguishable from those effects of 'contagion' and 'suggestion' which characterise crowd psychologies.[34] Mimetic desire is thereby understood as the very medium of those transversal flows of affect which characterise any social situation not understood in the inherently individualist and hierarchical terms of orthodox psychoanalysis. Such a perspective offers an elegant way of understanding the complex dynamic of agency and subjectification which Hills shows to be characteristic of 'fan cultures', while providing a way of understanding even the most apparently individualist of cultural formations – those focussed on a fascination with celebrities – as necessarily subtended by an affective infrastructure of transversal sociality.

Ethical evaluations: celebrity and democracy

However, such an account is not without problems. In particular, it runs the risk of producing a theoretical framework which inevitably generates optimistic readings of given cultural phenomena. If even celebrity culture is in fact the product of a democratic, transversal cultural productivity on the part of its participants, then everything is just groovy in the world of contemporary media culture, right? It is precisely the danger of such an implicit political complacency which critics object to in the work of commentators such as Fiske, and it is one which must obviously be avoided. Clearly, we need to try to respond to Hills's call for an approach to such issues which can go beyond any simplistic condemnation or valorisation.[35] Such a position must take account of the two broadly opposed positions on the nature of celebrity and sociality which we have already looked at. On the one hand, we have the psychoanalytic account which understands celebrity culture in terms of the individualised identifications which fans make with celebrities. On the other hand, we have a broadly deconstructive account which sees celebrity culture as generated at least partially by the transversal affective relations existing *between* its participants. There are two problems here, however, problems which might only be solved by building some bridges between these two accounts. Firstly, neither of these explanatory models has given us a very clear position from which to make any meaningful ethical or political comment on contemporary celebrity culture. If all we end up with is a meticulous speculative description of the psychodynamics of a given cultural formation, then it is not clear that we will have achieved anything worthwhile. Secondly, the fact is that the second account as we have rendered it thus far offers no real explanation for the historical specificities of that culture today.

Insofar as these two analytical frameworks would offer distinctive ethico-political positions, each would probably make some claim to speak in the name of democracy. The Lacanian models described above have all been associated at certain times with the 'radical democratic' political philosophy of Ernesto Laclau and Chantal Mouffe.[36] The position which appears to be more-or-less shared by Laclau, Mouffe, Zizek and Salecl is roughly as follows. Any 'society' (indeed, any discursive structure whatsoever) is characterised by the presence of that 'Master' whom Salecl describes as indispensable. The Master may take the form of an individual, an idea or a term: what is invariable is not its form but its function as 'master signifier'. What this master signifier always does is at least partially to disguise the fact that the place it occupies is empty: a hole which it may try to fill, but for which in fact it is only ever a screen. In fact, no structure can ever be fully self-enclosed, self-present and self-identical, and yet the persistence of all such structures is to some extent motivated by the drive to achieve the 'absent fullness' which such closure – and only such closure – would achieve. Most societies require at least symbolic (i.e. public, behavioural) submission to some figure of authority, some symbol, some stated ideal or creed: the ideal example would be the pledge of allegiance to the US flag sworn each morning by American school children. What distinguishes democracy from other forms of government is that it recognises the emptiness of that empty place which the master-signifier occupies. It does so implicitly and formally – if not always explicitly – precisely by making a space of public debate and contestation out of the central locus of decision-making in the society. In allowing a perpetual contest to go on at the heart of the power structure, it effectively recognises that that 'empty place' of power can never – and *should* never – be finally and ultimately filled.

From the alternative, deconstructive perspective which I have been developing here, this account leaves out an indispensable element. For this purely negative and formal account of 'democracy' finally says nothing about the *positive* conditions of democracy, and nothing about the crucial question of what democracy might actually feel like for its participants. Further to this, I would argue that if the term 'radical democracy' is to have any but a deliberately ironic meaning, and to keep any faith whatsoever with a socialist tradition which stretches back at least to the work of the 17th century political theorist Gerard Winstanley, then it must apply to a project for the deepening and extension of democratic social relations as well as for the formal designation of democratic political relations. In these terms, I would suggest that a certain horizontality of relations between members of a group is necessary for that group to be considered in any way democratic, and that the possibility of an 'affective tie'[37] *between* individuals (and possibly preceding their individuation as such) is a necessary precondition of any democratic community.

So how might these two perspectives generate ethical or political perspectives on contemporary celebrity culture? Radical Democratic political theory is in fact notoriously quiet on the politics of 'culture': despite the fact that each and every one of its theoretical sources independently supports the view that the field of formal 'Politics' is only one small part of the overall field of contested power relations, it tends to confine its attentions entirely to the narrow field of electoral and 'social movement' politics. However, there is nothing to prevent us from transposing the logic of its arguments concerning one field to a consideration of another. In this case, it seems that the emergence of celebrity culture might actually be seen as an inevitable and perhaps even a welcome concomitant of the general democratisation of society and culture. For if 'the master' – the irreducible point of common identification – is inevitably necessary in the formation of any collectivity whatsoever, and the democratic imperative is to render the space occupied by the master as empty as possible, to allow for a pluralistic proliferation of views and identities, then what could be more appropriate or desirable than that the stable and fixed – hence apparently consistent, authoritative and 'real' – 'masters' of earlier, more stable societies be replaced by the clearly two-dimensional and provisional 'masters' of celebrity culture? As discussed earlier, the celebrity is always aware – as is her public –

that her status depends on no divine right to rule the cultural sphere, but on her continued usefulness for her public as a support for their self-sustaining fantasies. The field of celebrity culture is a field in which the discursive contest over the *imagos* which we all need to render ourselves subjects is laid bare as just that – a discursive contest between candidates for imaginary authority, candidates to whom – unlike in earlier ages – we attribute no divine power or unchallengeable authority.

This may sound like an outlandish conclusion – that in fact celebrity culture is the product of a democratisation of the sphere of public culture – but there are serious reasons for supporting it. Firstly, there is the fact that the very latest manifestations of this phenomenon deliberately and self-consciously adopt the techniques of formal democracy. TV shows abound which invite the public to elect the winners of contests for a prize which is in general *nothing more or less than celebrity itself*: *Big Brother*, offering its contestants a derisory cash prize in return for months of public psychological torture, clearly derives its fascination for players and public from its dramatisation of the psychic relationship between celebrity and public, offering members of the public the chance to become celebrities for having done nothing more than successfully subject themselves to a ritualised version of the routines of privacy-invasion and popularity-poll which are the basic mechanisms of 'celebrification'.[38] Programmes like *Pop Idol*, *Fame Academy* and *I'm a Celebrity, Get me Out of Here* all involve the public electing their favourites from a field of existing or potential celebrities. Notoriously, so conventional wisdom has it, more people voted for the winner of the third series of *Big Brother* than for Tony Blair in the 2001 general election.

Secondly, both of the major studies of celebrity which I have already cited draw this conclusion, and even do so in terms which echo those of writers such as Salecl and Laclau. Rojek writes, in the final paragraph of his book:

> It is an enormous paradox that democracy, the system which claimed moral superiority on the basis of extending equality and freedom to all, cannot proceed without creating celebrities who stand above the common citizen and achieve veneration and god-like worship. It is easy to deplore this state of affairs, as Pierre Bourdieu does in his sally against media celebrities. But it is also rash to do so. Celebrity culture is the expression of a social form. As long as democracy and capitalism prevail there will always be an Olympus, inhabited not by Zeus and his court, but by celebrities, elevated from the mass, who embody the restless, fecund and frequently disturbing form of the mass in the public fact they assemble.[39]

The tone of this passage is strikingly resonant with Salecl's claim that 'there must always be a master'. Now, this is not to say that this new situation is necessarily a desirable one from the point of view of psychoanalysis. From Zizek's perspective,

Rojek's polytheistic imagery (and mine) would no doubt be telling. There is a long tradition in psychoanalytic thought, of which Zizek's pro-Christian writings are the latest example, of regarding the emergence of monotheism as a crucial stage in the development of the modern, rational subject, capable of understanding and acting on the world through science or politics.[40] In these terms, the rise of the new Pantheon of celebrities, like the decline of the Big Other, might be a worrisome condition of a general decline in the capacity of individuals to achieve the fully autonomous and rational subjectivity of which first monotheism and then Enlightenment (in the Kantian, rather than Vedic sense) were necessary conditions.

However, such commentary generally displays little to no commitment to democratisation as an ongoing political project, at best acknowledging the very limited forms of liberal democracy as being preferable to some forms of authoritarianism. It certainly seems at this stage in the argument that, on its own terms, a Lacanian Radical Democracy must either welcome the rise of celebrity culture as a inevitable feature of democracy, or disparage it for precisely the same reason.

Remarkably, Marshall's book concludes in a very similar way to Rojek's. The final section of the concluding chapter begins:

> I have argued that celebrities are manifestations of the organization of culture in terms of democracy and capitalism. They are the privileged form of what I have called public subjectivity. Their privilege is partly related to their capacity to act as discursive vehicles for the expression of such key ideologies as individuality or new consumer collective identities. In that capacity to house a discourse on individuality, celebrities, as I have noted, are intense sites for determining the meaning and significance of the private sphere and its implications for the public sphere. Fundamentally, celebrities represent the disintegration of the distinction between the private and the public.[41]

It is intriguing to compare this description of the emergence of celebrity culture with Laclau's 1990 comment that 'it is in the multiplication of "public spaces" and their constituencies beyond those accepted by classical liberalism that the base for the construction of a radical alternative lies.'[42] If the rise of celebrity culture is in part a process of making-public elements of the lives of rich and powerful individuals which were once consigned to the private sphere, then once again we have good reason for seeing this as an inherently democratic process.

Celebrity capitalism

Now, I hope that at this stage the reader is feeling a little uncomfortable. There is a widespread intuition that there is at least 'something wrong' with celebrity culture and 'celebritism' – that their shallow form of individualism is not something which we ought to welcome or encourage, and that there are reasons for resisting it beyond any support we may wish to express for traditional structures of authority and power. I do not think that we can actually conclude that celebrity culture is a welcome symptom of cultural democratisation. But I do want to point out the relative difficulty of explaining why this should be the case from the point of view of a formalist psychoanalytic understanding of democracy. Without any positive conception of democracy, a conception which acknowledges a certain radical sociality as constitutive of human culture and which recognises the centrality of the affective dimension to all politics, then it is not possible to say what it is, from a democratic perspective, that is wrong with celebritism at all.

However, there is still much which can be said from such a perspective which is useful. Of particular relevance is Chantal Mouffe's recent mobilisation of Carl Schmitt's criticism of the tendency to conflate liberalism with democracy. In a nutshell, Schmitt/Mouffe argues that liberal democracy was a historically contingent articulation of two discourses whose long-term compatibility was never very probable: the individualist discourse of liberalism and the democratic discourse of popular sovereignty being fundamentally impossible to reconcile.[43] Extrapolating from this view, it can be argued that liberalism is inherently bound up with the progress of capitalist social relations. Liberalism, as has long been acknowledged, is the political expression of that 'possessive individualism' which is the core ideology of capitalism.[44] Hence today the global hegemony of neo-liberal politico-economic regimes goes hand-in-hand with both the deep individualisation and the welcome social liberalisation characteristic of contemporary post-modern culture.

On the other hand, the 'Democratic Revolution'[45] – the process which sees collective public-decision-making extend both its constituency and its provenance from the end of the Renaissance to the late 20th century – depended always upon the mobilisation of collectivities understood as ethically and ontologically prior to the individuals of whom they are composed. What must emerge from this account is an implicit criticism of both Rojek and Marshall, who in their shared reference to 'democracy and capitalism', enact just the conflation which Mouffe deconstructs. It is not democracy in general but liberal democracy which they refer to, and a moment's reflection makes clear that in fact it is the 'liberal' element of the liberal-democracy copula which is central to their explanations. It is capitalist individualism, not democracy at all, which Rojek's, Marshall's and my analyses show to be at the heart of celebrity culture.

It is in recognising this fact that both of the problems identified earlier can be addressed. The 'deconstructive' model which I have offered as an alternative to the psychoanalytic one would clearly make a negative judgement about the nature and implications of contemporary celebrity culture on the grounds of its mutual imbrication with that individualistic 'common sense' which it opposes. Consider the remainder of David Marshall's conclusion:

> Fundamentally, celebrities represent the disintegration of the distinction between the private and the public. This disintegration, as represented by celebrities, has taken on a particular form. The private sphere is constructed to be revelatory, the ultimate site of truth and meaning for any representation in the public sphere. In a sense, the representation of public action as manifestation of private experience exemplifies a cultural pattern of psychologisation of the public sphere. The formation of a public subject is reduced to various psychological motivations, pressures at the micro level, the expression of family interest and personality traits.
>
> The celebrity is the avant-garde of the movement to vivisect public action by identifying the originary private experience. It functions as a discursive vehicle that reduces the cultural meaning of events, incidents and people to their psychological makeup. The celebration of affective attachment to events and moments is represented by the celebrity, where further cultural connections are dematerialized. The celebrity can be seen as instrumental in the organisation of an affective economy.
>
> The affective economy, where there is a reduction of meaning to psychological motivations, has become central to the way in which politics and culture operate. Daniel Bell's famous expression of the end of ideology in the 1950s can be reread as the rise and celebration of affective meaning. Similarly, the end of the Cold War can be reread as the end of the effort to fabricate social meaning and the elevation of the moments of feeling that are provided by an affective economy.
>
> Celebrities, as the affective economy's construction of public individuals, are sites for the dispersal of power and meaning into the personal and therefore universal. They represent the reorganization of collective identities into the affective economy of the contemporary capitalist democracy.[46]

This passage clarifies many issues, but it is itself in need of some clarification. Firstly, it suggest that what is taking place is emphatically not a 'multiplication of "public spaces"' but the reverse: a kind of privatisation of the public. However, this distinction can only be made if we overcome Marshall's persistent conflation of individualism with democracy. It is not 'democracy', capitalist or otherwise, to which this privatisation is central, but a certain neo-liberal psycho-political formation which is entirely non-democratic in character insofar as it increasingly forecloses any possibility of real popular sovereignty. What Marshall refers to as 'contemporary capitalist democracy' would be better understood as what Colin Crouch calls 'post-democracy': a set of political arrangements which may retain the procedural characteristics of representative democracy but which are unable to give any meaningful expression to popular wills which might conflict with the demands of capital.[47] Marshall also tends to conflate 'affective' with 'personal': in contrast to this I would emphasise the centrality to a deconstructive social-ist account of an understanding of 'affect' as, in Brian Massumi's words 'a prepersonal intensity'.[48] Indeed, this conflation of the affective with the personal can be understood as itself symptomatic of the very situation which Marshall diagnoses. Furthermore, both the conflation of the affective with the personal and the mobilisation of an affective economy based on this conflation are absolutely typical of an 'Oedipalised society' as understood by Deleuze and Guattari.

It is here that we come to the point where we can solve the other problem which we identified above. The deconstructive social-ist framework outlined above lacks a historical dimension only if we overlook the contribution which Deleuze and Guattari's distinctive historiography can make to it. At the same time, a proper consideration of this aspect of their work can actually make possible a reconciliation between it and the work of figures such as Zizek and Laclau. Contrary to some received opinion, Deleuze and Guattari do not simply dispute the veracity of all psychoanalytic explanation. Rather, they assert that the Oedipus complex – Freud's key posited mechanism of individuation – must be understood as a historically specific mode of subjectification, the product of the interrelationship of capitalism with a particular 'regime of signs':[49]

> Yes, Oedipus is universal. But the error lies in having believed in the following alternative: either Oedipus is the product of the social repression-psychic repression system, in which case it is not universal; or it is universal, and a position of desire. In reality, it is universal because it is the displacement of the limit that haunts all societies, the displaced represented that disfigures what all societies dread: namely, the decoded flows of desire.
>
> This is not to say that the universal Oedipal limit is 'occupied', strategically occupied in all social formations. We must take Kardiner's remark seriously: a Hindu or an Eskimo can dream of Oedipus, without however being subjected to the complex, without 'having the complex'. For Oedipus to be occupied, a certain number of social conditions are indispensable: the field of social production and reproduction must become independent of familial reproduction, that is, independent of the territorial machine [i.e. tribal social structures] that declines alliances and filiations.[50]
>
> We have seen in what sense schizophrenia was the *absolute limit* of every society, inasmuch as it sets in motion decoded and deterritorialized flows that it restores to desiring-production. And capitalism, the *relative limit* of every society, inasmuch as it axiomitizes the decoded flows and reterritorializes the deterritorialized flows. We have also found that capitalism finds in

schizophrenia its own *exterior limit*, which it is continually repelling and exorcising, while capitalism itself produces its *immanent limits*, which it never ceases to displace and enlarge. But capitalism still needs a displaced *interior limit* in another way: precisely in order to neutralize or repel the exterior limit, the schizophrenic limit; it needs to internalize this limit this time by restricting it, by causing it to pass no longer between social production and the desiring-production that breaks away from social production, between the form of social reproduction and the form of a familial reproduction to which social production is reduced, between the social aggregate and the private subaggregate to which the social aggregate is applied.

Oedipus is this displaced or internalised limit where desire lets itself be caught. …It is only in the capitalist formation that Oedipus finds itself not only occupied, but inhabited and lived…It is not via a flow of shit or a wave of incest that Oedipus arrives, but via the decoded flows of capital-money.[51]

So, capitalism – and, more specifically, *currency* – is understood as that which brings Oedipus in its wake.

Small faces

This implicit reference to currency – without which there can clearly be no 'decoded flows of capital-money' – refers us back to the beginning of this essay, and the observation that it was the coinage of the ancient world which represented the very first medium of celebrification as the becoming-recognised of a face. This in itself draws our attention to Deleuze and Guattari's notoriously complex meditations on what they term 'faciality'.[52] For Deleuze and Guattari, the face is itself a particular means of mapping/materialising the self-body which only acquires significance in a society characterised by particular modes of individualisation. 'Primitive' peoples, they contend, do not have 'faces' in the modern sense, communicating through a much wider repertoire of somatic and sonic gestures, marking their bodies in complex significatory ways. To simplify greatly, the 'face' as a socio-personal institution would seem to be, for Deleuze and Guattari, tied up with the emergence of the Western 'rational' self-enclosed subject, rather as Derrida sees the purity and self-presence of the signifying voice as central to the maintenance of the Western philosophical imaginary.[53]

Significantly, Deleuze and Guattari describe the face as a deterritorialization/reterritorialization of the body. Now, we can relate this view to our remarks about currency as the substance of deterritorialized capital by considering another point at which Deleuze and Guattari discuss the significance of the face. Describing the 'regime of signs' which organises those very despotic-imperial societies which minted the first coins, as the 'signifying regime', Deleuze and Guattari implicitly identify the historical moment of the birth of coinage with that of the birth of those discursive structures which psychoanalysis understands as universal and largely ahistorical. Of course, Deleuze and Guattari never mention coins, but they clearly imply that the situation understood by psychoanalysis (and in this case that includes Lacan, Zizek and Laclau) whereby a field of signification is composed of a network of signs each referring to each other and sustained in its systematicity by the presence of one 'master signifier' is in fact a situation only fully pertaining within the despotic regime of signs, within which the role of the infinitely interpretative role of the psychoanalyst was once taken by the despot-god's priests.

Writing of the status of the 'master signifier' within such a regime, Deleuze and Guattari say

> There is not much to say about the centre of signifiance, or the Signifier in person, because it is a pure abstraction no less than a pure principle; in other words, it is nothing. Lack or excess, it hardly matters. It comes to the same thing to say that the sign refers to other signs ad infinitum and that the infinite set of all signs refers to a supreme signifier. At any rate, this pure formal redundancy of the signifier could not even be conceptualised if it did not have its own substance of expression, for which we must find a name: *faciality*. Not only is language always accompanied by faciality traits, but the face crystallises all redundancies, it emits and receives, releases and recaptures signifying signs. It is a whole body unto itself: it is like the body of the centre of significance to which all of the deterritorialized signs affix themselves, and it marks the limit of their deterritorialization…The signifier is always facialised…The despot-god has never hidden his face, far from it: he makes himself one, or even several …With the despot, everything is public, and everything that is public is so by virtue of the face.[54]

Although Deleuze and Guattari later associate the rise of faciality with that of Christanity, with their reference to 'Jesus Christ Superstar'[55] precisely implying that the Christian facial regime functions by rendering Jesus as the ultimate celebrity, here they identify it with just those pre-Christian imperial theocracies which were, in fact, the first societies to decorate coins with the faces of real people.

A number of observations converge here. In a slight but significant revision of Deleuze and Guattari, we must acknowledge that the deterritorialization of the despotic face begins at exactly the moment of its greatest power, in a process by which the face will deterritorialize first the body of the despot-god (extending its power immeasurably while at the same time, indissolubly, de-materializing it and destabilising it) and then that of every Western subject, eventually undermining even the Oedipal structures which emerge at one point in the history of passage from one state of 'civilisation' to another. The first cult of celebrity – of the recognised-face – is the cult of the emperor, and the means of ensuring that recognition is coinage. Yet coinage is the very medium of deterritorialized capital, the substance of the flow which the despotic and feudal regimes will do their best to contain, and ultimately will fail to do so. If Oedipus as understood by Freud is effectively the residual-conjunctural product of one specific moment in this history, then this leaves us with an account derived from Deleuze and Guattari which would not ultimately be incompatible at all with that offered by Zizek. Today, the proliferation of celebrity culture is an effect and a symptom of this long history, a history which begins at the moment when the very earliest forms of capitalism begin to dissolve the socio-symbolic structures out of which they are born, and which today manifests itself in a culture of superficial visuality, frantic personalisation and deep individualism: a facialised, subjectified, post-Oedipal culture in which the only constant is the capacity of capital flows and the seemingly infinite imperialism of market relations to disrupt all stable structures while demanding ever-greater degrees of submission to the law which demands that each of us be a subject, a commodity, a person, an in-dividual, a face.

So how to respond to this situation, without resorting to the normative conservatism of the psychoanalysts? While warning against the real dangers of primitivism, regression and actual psychosis, Deleuze and Guattari recommend a strategy aimed at dissolving the fixity and individuality of facialised subjects: 'Become clandestine, make rhizome everywhere'[56] must be the ultimate anti-celebretist statement. Are there concrete examples of such practices? One which springs to mind, although by now it's a cliché, is the well-documented refusal of house and techno artists since the 1990s to release records under consistent monikers, or to depict themselves on record covers or in publicity material: a deliberate refusal of the culture of celebrity in favour of a focus on the affective flows of force and sound which constitute dance-floor collectivities and can never be tied down by faces, names, music-industry careers.[57] As is now well known, the mobilisation of opportunistic and politically uncommitted DJs as the stars of dance culture in the late 1990s was largely motivated by the insistence of the press that they had to have *faces* to put on their covers. Across the music press the selection or refusal of a design aesthetic which focuses on the face, hence on the production of celebrity, is a sure index of a publication's complicity with or refusal of hegemonic norms. Graphic covers, we are told, never sell as well as ones depicting stars, or even potential stars, no matter how avant-garde the music under discussion.[58]

As limited a sphere as this is, there's no reason why it shouldn't be a model for others. Only a deliberate refusal to participate in the endless cycle of facialisation, celebrification, personalisation, individualisation will upset the workings of the abstract machine of celebrity, but such refusals can be effective, as the micro-history of dance culture attests. It may well be, if the history of celebrity is the history of money, which is the history of capital's entire long adventure of creative destruction, that only such strategies, which deliberately refuse the commodification and personalisation of knowledges and affects, can stand against this force. Would this have any meaning for other kinds of cultural work, even academic work? One implication might be to declare once again the death of Authors: aren't authors the celebrities of academic culture, after all? If refusing to think of music in terms of names and faces is effective (and it is), then why not talk about ideas in the same way. Shut up about Derrida – let's talk about deconstruction. Shut up about Deleuze – let's talk about schizoanalysis. Stop dreaming of being a star in the university marketplace, a brand, a commodity sold to the highest bidder. Write collectively under assumed names. Distribute for free on the internet.

Ultimately, of course, this is all already known. What characterises the new and dynamic forms of politics which are emerging in the struggle against neoliberalism is precisely their instantiation of an ethic of collective creativity, horizontal organisation, and participative experience. In its most concrete, unpoetic form, an innovation such as the famous participatory budget in Porto Allegre can be seen as manifesting the same deconstructive social-ist ethic which I've been working towards here. The Workers' Party attempt to allow the people of this Brazilian city to meet in a truly public way, to discuss and decide the economic future of their town, has inspired others all around the world precisely because it is the antithesis of a post-democratic political system based on the culture of celebrity ('vote for him – he seems like a nice guy…'). It's not a new idea, that the struggle for democracy – real democracy, radical democracy – depends upon a mobilisation of the transversal multitude,[59] on an assertion of the creative and liberatory potential of the social against the capitalist drive to privatise and personalise; but at a time when we are encouraged in more ways than ever to equate individualisation with social progress, it needs asserting more than ever. Unless our theoretical models and interventions can lend support to such a project – instead of, like many forms of contemporary psychoanalytic theorising, implicitly denying its very possibility – then they will be part of the problem and not part of the solution.

Notes

All websites accessed July 2003.

1. P. David Marshall, *Celebrity and Power*, University of Minnesota Press, Minneapolis 1997.
2. http://www.phil.frb.org/education/medcoin.html; http://members.verizon.net/vze3xycv/Jerusalem/confPotlSelu.htm
3. Alexander Garcia Düttmann, *Between Cultures: Tensions in the Struggle for Recognition*, Verso, London 2000.
4. G.W.F. Hegel, *Phenomenology of Spirit*, Clarendon Press, Oxford, 1977. The phrases 'master' and 'slave' are often translated differently: as, for example, 'Lord' and 'Bondsman'.
5. John Fiske, *Television Culture*, Routledge, London and New York 1987.

6. The most explicit, but also the most intellectually rigorous, representative of the anti-Fiske industry is Jim McGuigan, *Cultural Populism*, Routledge, London 1992.
7. Marshall, op cit, p65.
8. Chris Rojek, *Celebrity*, Reaktion Books, London 2001, p95.
9. Ibid, p95.
10. Ibid, p97.
11. Georg Simmel, 'The Metropolis and Mental Life' in *Simmel on Culture*, edited by David Frisby and Mike Featherstone, Sage, London 1997.
12. Ulrich Beck and Elisabeth Beck-Gernsheim, *Individualization*, Sage, London 2002.
13. Zygmunt Bauman, *The Individualized Society*, Polity 2001.
14. Fredric Jameson, *Postmodernism or The Cultural Logic of Late Capitalism*, Verso, London 2001.
15. See, for example, http://www.bowlingalone.com/.
16. Ernesto Laclau, 'Identity and Hegemony' in Butler, Laclau, Zizek, *Contingency, Hegemony, Universality*, Verso, London 2000, p57.
17. This is a translation of the French *méconnaissance*, which is conventionally rendered in French in English translations of Lacan, e.g. Jacques Lacan, *Écrits*, Routledge, London 1977, p6.
18. Laclau, op cit, p55.
19. Sigmund Freud, 'On Narcissism' in *On Metapsychology*, Penguin, London 1984, pp86-97; 'Group Psychology and the Analysis of the Ego' in *Civilisation, Society and Religion*, Penguin, London 1985, pp134-40.
20. Ulrich Beck, Antony Giddens and Scott Lasch, *Reflexive Modernization*, Polity, Cambridge, 1994.
21. Slavoj Zizek, *The Ticklish Subject: The Absent Centre of Political Ontology*, Verso 1999, p334.
22. Manuel Castells, *The Power of Identity*, Blackwell, Oxford 1997.
23. Zizek, op cit, p334.
24. Ibid, p366-9.
25. Marshall, op cit, pp27-50.
26. Renata Salecl, *The Spoils of Freedom: psychoanalysis and feminism after the fall of socialism*, Routledge, London 1994, p140.
27. Gilles Deleuze & Félix Guattari, *A Thousand Plateaus*, trans. Brian Massumi, Athlone, London 1988, p341.
28. Alan O'Shea, 'English Subjects of Modernity' in Nava & O'Shea (eds) *Modern Times*, Routledge, London 1996.
29. Gilles Deleuze & Félix Guattari, *Anti-Oedipus*, trans. Hurley et al, University of Minnesota Press, Minneapolis 1983, p280.
30. Most tellingly, this was true even where commentators were drawing on theoretical sources very close to those being mobilised here. See http://muse.jhu.edu/journals/theory_&_event/v001/ for the most striking examples. The nearest exceptions were to be found in articles by Carol Watt and Mark Gibson in *New Formations 36: Diana and Democracy*, Lawrence & Wishart, London 1999.
31. Matt Hills, *Fan Cultures*, Routledge, London 2002, pp170-1.
32. René Girard, *The Girard Reader*, edited by James G. Williams, Crossroad Herder, New York 1996, pp33-44; 225-242.
33. Mikkel Borch-Jacobsen, *The Freudian Subject*, trans. Catherine Porter, Stanford University Press, Stanford 1988, p26.
34. Ibid, pp127-239.
35. Hills, op cit.
36. Ernesto Laclau and Chantal Mouffe, *Hegemony and Socialist Strategy*, Verso, London 1985.

37. Mikkel Borch-Jacobsen, *The Emotional Tie*, trans. Catherine Porter, Stanford University Press, Stanford 1992. I would strongly suggest that a more accurate translation of the French title – *Le Lien Affectif* – would be *The Affective Tie*. This issue relates directly to the persistent controversy over the correct translation of Spinoza's *affectum*. In general, the radical, Deleuzian tradition insists on the specificity of the term/concept 'affect' as designating a transmission of force/power – not simply an individualised emotional state – while a more conservative tradition, including object-relations psychoanalysis, uses the terms 'emotion' and 'affect' interchangeably, reducing the latter term to a synonym of the former.
38. Rojek, op cit.
39. Ibid, pp198-9.
40. Sigmund Freud, 'Moses and Monotheism' in *The Origins of Religion*, Penguin, London 1985; Julia Kristeva, *Tales of Love*, trans. Leon S. Roudiez, Columbia University Press, New York 1987, pp103-21; Slavoj Zizek, *The Fragile Absolute*, Verso, London 2000.
41. Marshall, op cit, pp246-7.
42. Ernesto Laclau, *New Reflections on the Revolution of Our Times*, Verso, London 1990, pxv.
43. Chantal Mouffe, *The Democratic Paradox*, Verso, London 2000, pp36-59.
44. See C.B. MacPherson, *The Political Theory of Possessive Individualism*, Clarendon Press, Oxford 1964.
45. Claude Lefort, *L'Invention Démocratique*, Fayard, Paris 1994, p172.
46. Marshall, op cit, p247.
47. Colin Crouch, *Coping with Post-Democracy*, Fabian Society, London 2000.
48. Deleuze and Guattari, *A Thousand Plateaus*, Translator's notes, pxvi.
49. Ibid, pp111-148.
50. Deleuze and Guattari, *Anti-Oedipus* p177.
51. Ibid, pp266-7.
52. For a highly lucid discussion see Ronald Bogue, *Deleuze on Music, Painting and the Arts*, Routledge, New York 2003.
53. Jacques Derrida, *Of Grammatology*, trans. G. Spivak, John Hopkins University Press, Baltimore 1974.
54. Deleuze and Guattari, *A Thousand Plateaus*, p115.
55. Ibid, p176.
56. Ibid, p91.
57. Jeremy Gilbert and Ewan Pearson, *Discographies*, London, Routledge, 1999; Simon Reynolds, *Energy Flash*, Picador, London 1998.
58. For example, *The Wire* magazine signalled its shift in policy away from a sophisticated post-modern radicalism to a more conservative, masculinist avant-gardism in the mid-1990s by substituting a graphics-driven aesthetic for one which uniformly focussed on the face, a single – almost always male, white – cover star. While this was the aesthetic shared by almost all UK music publications during the 1990s, the most politically and intellectually innovative magazine of the period – *The Lizard* – eschewed it entirely throughout its predictably short life.
59. See Michael Hardt and Antonio Negri, *Empire*, Harvard University Press, Cambridge 2000.

Guidelines for Contributors

Each issue is planned around a theme. Prospective writers are encouraged to contact the editor to discuss their ideas. Please keep in mind that we aim for an accessible style of writing, free of jargon and aimed at communicating with a general non-fiction audience as well as academic and student markets. The titles of articles and general phrasing should avoid academic orthodoxy.

Keep references to a minimum. Notes should be used for referencing sources, rather than indicating other books or essays in the same field. They should be numbered in the Chicago style, using superscript. All notes should be placed at the end of the article.

No Bibliographies.

Essays should be between 4,000 and 6,000 words long. Please post one copy to

> Jonathan Rutherford, Editor
> *Mediactive*
> Media Communications and Cultural Studies
> Middlesex University
> White Hart Lane
> London N17 8HR

Send an email attachment in Word to J.rutherford@mdx.ac.uk or to the issue editor. Please include:

1. A 100-word synopsis to introduce the article. This will appear on the first page of the article, after the title;
2. A couple of sentences to describe yourself, for inclusion on the notes on contributors page.

Copyright

Submissions of a paper to *Mediactive* will be taken to imply that it presents original, unpublished work not under consideration for publication elsewhere. By submitting a manuscript the author agrees that he or she is granting the Publisher for a fixed term the exclusive right to reproduce and distribute the paper including reprints, photographic reproductions, microfilm or any other reproduction of a similar nature, and translations. He or she will not be required to assign the copyright.

Notes

Use a superscript number in the text. Each reference should follow this basic format: name, *book*, publisher date.

Note the commas. Book in italics, no brackets around publisher. p6, not p.6 or p. 6; pp67-69 not pp. 67-69 or pp.67-69; op cit not op. cit.; ibid not ibid.

A more detailed version of this guide is available from the editor and will be sent out to contributors. Please check your copy against the guide before sending it to the editor.

Notes on Contributors

Anita Biressi is Senior Lecturer in Cultural and Media Studies at Roehampton, University of Surrey. Publications include: 'An Englishman's Home...Reflections on the Tony Martin Case' (with Heather Nunn) in *Soundings* July 2002, 'Silent Witness: Detection, Femininity and the Post-mortem Body' (with Heather Nunn) in *Feminist Media Studies* (forthcoming) and *Crime, Fear and the Law in True Crime Stories*, Palgrave, London/New York, 2001. She is currently co-writing a book with Heather Nunn on Reality Television for Wallflower Press.

Kay Dickinson lectures in Film Studies at King's College, University of London. She is the editor of *Movie Music, The Film Reader* (Routledge, 2003) and *Teen TV* (bfi, forthcoming).

Jeremy Gilbert teaches Cultural Studies at the University of East London. He is the co-author of *Discographies: Dance Music, Culture, and the Politics of Sound* (Routledge 1999) and the co-editor of *Cultural Capitalism: Politics after New Labour* (Lawrence & Wishart 2000), and has contributed to various journals and edited collections.

Matt Hills is the author of *Fan Cultures* (Routledge, 2002) and co-editor of *Intensities: The Journal of Cult Media* (www.cult-media.com). He is currently completing *The Pleasures of Horror* (Continuum, forthcoming) and has recently contributed to *Red Noise: Buffy the Vampire Slayer and TV Studies* (Duke University Press, forthcoming) and *The TV Studies Reader* (Routledge, forthcoming). Matt is a lecturer in Media and Cultural Studies at Cardiff University.

Jo Littler teaches Media and Cultural Studies at Middlesex University. She is currently co-editing a book with Roshi Naidoo entitled *The politics of heritage: the legacies of 'race'* (Routledge, forthcoming 2004).

Heather Nunn is Senior Lecturer in Cultural Studies at Roehampton, University of Surrey. Publications include 'Violence and the Sacred: the iron lady, the Princess and the people's PM' in *New Formations* 1999 No.36 and 'Running Wild: Fictions of Gender and Childhood in Thatcher's Britain' in *EnterText* Summer 2002. Her book *Thatcher, Politics and Fantasy: The Political Culture of Gender and Nation* was published by Lawrence and Wishart in 2003. She is currently co-writing a book with Anita Biressi on Reality Television for Wallflower Press.

Oscar Reyes is a PhD candidate on the Ideology and Discourse Analysis Programme, University of Essex. His current and forthcoming publications are on New Labour's family politics, populism, and the theory of ideology.

Past and future issues

Mediactive bridges the gap between universities and public debate, engaging with contemporary issues of politics and culture; it uses theoretical concepts, but tries to be free of jargon – aiming at a general non-fiction readership as well as an academic market. The principle idea is the fast and effective publication of good quality writing and scholarly work, and the use of modern technologies to reduce costs to a minimum.

Issue 1 Knowledge/Culture, edited by Jonathan Rutherford (autumn 2003)

Mediactive 1 looks at the revolutionary changes being made in the provision of public forms of education in the UK, largely instituted by policies informed by neoliberalism. The changes to practices of knowledge creation and academic life are paradigmatic, and we need to understand these new conditions, and to create a language and politics which can reassert the value of knowledge and education as public goods. The issue includes: an analysis of the nature of knowledge; discussion on New Labour and the knowledge economy, cultural studies as an area of contestation, the commodification of education and news journalism; new thoughts on science and culture; and a rethinking of intellectual work in the digital age. **Contributors** Clare Birchall, Lynda Dyson, Alan Finlayson, Andrew Goffey, Gary Hall, Glenn Rikowski, Jonathan Rutherford.

The Mediawar Issue 3 Summer 2004

Issue 3 examines the media's portrayal of the Iraq war, and the media management that has become a central component of the military's war strategy. *Mediawar* analyses the ways in which issues of interpretation, meaning and representation in the coverage of war have become a constant site of political struggle. The issue includes discussion of: war reportage as entertainment; political activism and alternative war news; children and war coverage; the gendered representation of women at war; embedded journalists; media imperialism and 24/7 news; the future roles of mediawars. **Contributors** Anita Biressi, Cindy Carter, Maire Messenger Davies, Des Freedman, R. Harindranth, Pat Holland, Heather Nunn, Darren O'Byrne, Paul Rixon, Daya Thussu.

Issue 4 Asylum Autumn 2004

Issue 4 takes on asylum. What does the widespread circulation of hateful and racist representations of migrants, and the individual paranoia invoked by cultural difference, tell us about European cultures? Can we create a collective response to migration that is based on mutual give and take, and an ethic of concern for the other? The issue includes: the meaning of being a good neighbour; the dynamics of hate and xenophobia; the cashing-in of corporations; the politics of human security; refugees/asylum seekers as the coming *condition humaine*; ideas for a new European identity. **Contributors** Zygmunt Bauman, Rosemary Bechler, Farhad Dalal, Richard Payne, Jonathan Rutherford, Nira Yuval-Davis.

For further details and to buy copies: www.barefootpublications.co.uk